SQUADRONS, PATCHES, HERALDRY & ARTWORK OF THE INDIAN AIR FORCE
1932-2016

BY PHILLIP CAMP

ACKNOWLEDGEMENTS:

IAF HQ for arranging access to several airbases in the period 1996 till 2012.
Simon Watson, Jagan Pillarisetti, Vayu Aerospace Magazine, Peter Steinemann, Henny Putker, Vijay Seth, Atamvir Singh Multani, Sebastian Hoja.
IAF Official Website and IAF Website by Bharat Rakshak.
Eagles over Bangladesh by Jagan Pillarisetti and Samir Chopra, Harper Collins India 2013.
IAF Historical & Warrior Studies Cell, College of Air Warfare. Squadrons of the IAF series. (6)
Peacekeeping and Protection of Civilians. The IAF in the Congo by Air Cdr Rajesh Isser, Knowledge World 2012.
Spitfires in the Sun by Vikram Singh, USI 2014.
Squadron History books by the Society for Aerospace Studies. (1, 5, 7, 14, 20, 28, 47 and 221)
The Gnat in India, 1958-1991 by Pushpinder Singh.
The Eagle Strikes. History of the RIAF by Sqn Ldr R.T.S Chhina.
The Purple Legacy, IAF Helicopters in Service of the Nation by Air Cdr Rajesh Isser. Pentagon Press 2012.
The IAF at Eighty by Vijay Seth. Published by Seth Communications 2013.
Training Command by HQTC 2006.
So That Others May Live by IAF
Unarmed Into Battle by Atma Singh, Knowledgeworld 2012
Ceremonial Glimpses of the IAF by Wg Cdr R.K. Mandal, Ratana Books 2002.

And the following units who have kindly donated to the cause during visits;
1, 2, 3, 4, 6, 7, 8, 9, 10, 16, 20, 23, 24, 25, 27, 28, 29, 30, 31, 32, 35, 37, 47, 48, 52, 101, 108, 109, 112, 116, 125, 128, 129, 141, 151, 221, 223, 224, AFA, FTW, FWTF, HTS, MOFTU, OCU, ASTE, ADA, CABS, HAL.

Squadrons, Patches, Heraldry & Artwork of the Indian Air Force: 1932-2016
Published by Phillip Camp, The Aviation Bookshop

ISBN: 978-0-9559597-1-4

Words and images
© Phillip Camp

Design & Layout
© James Lawrence, Gingercake Creative – www.gingercake-creative.co.uk

Published by : Phillip Camp – email: philcamp@aerorepltd.co.uk

All rights reserved. No part of this publication may be reproduced, stored in a retrieval system, transmitted in any form or by any means, electronic, mechanical or photocopied, recorded or otherwise, without written permission of the author.

Printed in India by Replika Press Pvt. Ltd.,

CONTENTS

INTRODUCTION 5

FLYING SQUADRONS 9

HELICOPTER UNITS 147

NON NUMBERED FLYING UNITS 185

QUASI-MILITARY FLYING UNITS 239

MISCELLANEOUS 251

GLOSSARY 268

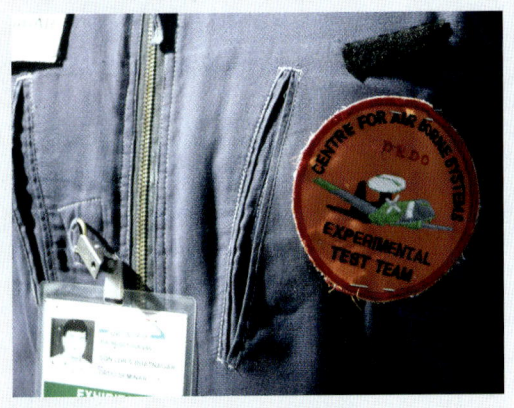

DEDICATION

This was my first Indian patch picked up at Aero India in 1996. It is picture here pinned to the flying suit of Sqn Ldr S. Bhatnagar, a test pilot for the Defence Research and Development Organisation (DRDO).

This book is dedicated to **Sqn Ldr S. Bhatnagar** who was sadly killed along with his crew whilst flying the Centre For Airborne Systems AWACS modified HS-748 at Arrakonam on 11th January 1999.

(see page 246 for more details)

INTRODUCTION

The IAF came into being on October 8th, 1932. Since then it has fought with distinction in a world war, a border skirmish with China and four wars with Pakistan. It has also served within the territorial borders of India as an aid to the civilian population especially with disaster relief and the opening up of remote areas. As an active participant within the UNO, they have committed aircraft to several peace keeping missions in Africa and Sri Lanka. Today they are one of the largest air forces in world having over 140 individual units flying a mixture of Western, Russian and Indigenous types. For the record several IAF squadrons served with distinction in the Burma campaign, being awarded the battle honours of;

South Burma 1942   Chindits Operations 1943
Maungdaw-Buthidaung 1944   Imphal 1944
Kaladan 1945   Kangaw Ramree 1945

Battle honours are given to recognise the fact that a unit fought creditably and with distinction beyond the call of duty against the enemy in a particular operation. Only operational squadrons/flights/units are eligible for the award of the battle honour. The President of India approved a series of Battle Honours in 1981 for campaigns and battles going back to WWII and up to the 1971 War. On 2nd December 1994, the President approved 24 Battle Honours to 20 different squadrons and units of the IAF.

This book aims to record as many patches and crests as possible from the flying units together with a brief resume of each unit, where known. Most from the original WWII squadrons were accepted by the Inspector of RAF Badges, under rules laid down by the English College of Arms and that had to go for final approval by King George VI. Upon India becoming a Republic, the crests were re-drafted to reflect their allegiance to the Government of India. The Crown was replaced by Ashoka Lions and the newly drafted design was then approved by the President of India.

All fighter and transport squadrons have enjoyed their identity for many years. Helicopter units on the other hand used a generic crest and motto for many years which have slowly been replaced by individualistic heraldry. The President Standard is awarded to a squadron or unit that completes 18 years in the IAF, or for appreciation of outstanding performance on operations. The design of the standard was approved on the 12th August 1961 and it consists of a blue silk flag, fringed and tasselled, measuring 4 feet by 2 feet 8 inches, within the fringe. The squadron's individual badge is centred on the background with scrolls either side which are meant for recording up to eight battle honours and this is surrounded by a border of Lotus flowers and Ashoka leaves.

5

PATCHES

I have collected patches for many years and during my first visit to India for Aero India in 1996, I was able to gather a few examples from surprised pilots who were attending the event. Since then my collection of Indian military aviation patches has reached in excess of 1000. Indian patches come in many forms. Basically things started off with hand stitched patches which tend to be more collectable and can still be found with some units today. Hand-made patches tended to be a cottage industry centred on two hotspots at Ambala Cantonment and the insignia making town of Malerkotla - both visited by me in search of patches.

You can also get those where the insignia is printed onto a cotton sheet in large quantity and then cut out for the on base tailor to add a plastic covering, Velcro back and edging. Many ground crews would also take these and just stitch them to their uniform without going through the tailoring process. Other unusual mediums are the use of metal and printed naugahyde patches which are not some common now. Nowadays Indian Pilots strive for the quality of the modern manufactured patch. In the 90's embroidered patches started to appear, but these have largely been superseded by computer designed images being manufactured on weaving machines. These predominantly consist of woven fabric which gives a better profile and written detail on the fabric, which is not possible on embroidered patches. These new style patches can be made to give an embroidered effect by adding Lurex Weave which can give a raised effect. The first rubber 3D effect patches started to appear in 2015.

Crests have been used for the purpose of recognition and distinguishing formations or units. The IAF has adopted various crests for Commands, Squadrons and other establishments. The IAF Crests comprise of a standard framework. The central position of the frame contains of the individual formation sign with the motto (usually in Sanskrit) shown on a scroll at the foot of the frame. The unit sign is drawn inside a circle of 3 ½ inches diameter. The name of the unit is shown in the upper half (usually in Hindi or English), while 'Bhartya Vayu Sena/Indian Air Force' is inscribed in the lower half. The Crest is approved by the President of India and is of great historical and sentimental value. The importance of the Crest can be understood from the fact that the movement of the Crest from one place to another is done by the hand of an officer.

▼ Badge making by hand in Merlakotla in 2008. At the time two MiG-29 squadrons were on detachment at nearby Halwara.

FLYING SQUADRONS

On becoming a Republic, the IAF was an eight squadron air force. An expansion plan in 1953 was introduced that would raise this to 15 squadrons, later rising to 25 following an Air Headquarters proposal to the Government of India (GOI). The proposal for 25 squadrons was approved in 1956 and the growth in strength of India's neighbours, necessitated another increase to a 33 squadron force in 1961. The 1962 and 1965 Wars, bought about a 5 year plan (1964-1969) which proposed an increase to 45 combat squadrons, plus additional transport and helicopter units. This figure was never achieved and recently the IAF set a goal of reaching 42 combat squadrons by 2027.

1 SQUADRON
'TIGERS'

▲ 1 sqn Mystere IV and pilot 1960's. They operated this aircraft between 1957 and 1966.

▼ Mirage 2000TH with Tiger Tanks to celebrate 75th anniversary of 1 Squadron at Gwalior 2008.

The first IAF squadron to be formed was 1 squadron at Drigh Road, Karachi on 1st April 1933 with the Westland Wapiti. By 1937 its three flights operated from various locations in the North West frontier province. In June 1939 they converted onto the Hawker Hart and Audax before getting the Westland Lysander in 1941. On 1st February 1942 they moved to Toungoo, 200 miles north of Rangoon, where their Lysanders saw operational service, including bombing Japanese Airfields. Later on they moved to Lashio and Mingaladon where they provided tactical reconnaissance and Army co-operation. In June 1942 they moved to Risalpur in order to convert onto the Hawker Hurricane I and returned to operations at Imphal in February 1944 after conversion to the Hurricane IIB. In the tactical reconnaissance role they flew 4813 operational sorties returning to Kohat on India's North Western frontier in April 1945. They converted onto the Supermarine Spitfire Mk.VIII in November 1945 and for a short time operated both the Hurricane and Spitfire. They received the Spitfire Mk.XIV in March 1947 before getting the Hawker Tempest II at Risalpur in May 1947. At the time of partition in 1947 the original No 1 squadron, Royal Indian Air Force was ceded to Pakistan and they were stood down on 14th August 1947. The squadron was reformed on 26th January

1953 at Halwara with Spitfire Mk.XVIIIe's passed down from 15 squadron and they quickly converted onto jets receiving the Vampire FB52. They moved to Palam and later Kalaikunda, where on 15th February 1957 they re-equipped with the Dassault Mystere IVA. Later they saw service in the Goa conflict of December 1961 and during the Indo Pakistan War of 1965 flying 174 sorties, of which 120 were strike missions, notably counter air strikes at Sargodha airbase. The squadron converted onto the MiG-21FL at Adampur between June and September 1966 and during the 1971 Indo Pakistan War their prime responsibility was the defence of Adampur and the surrounding north western Punjab. They provided escort to Su-7 strike missions, combat air patrols over Amritsar and Pathankot and finished the conflict having flown 518 sorties. Post 1971 they moved to Gorakhpur in 1984 and later to Hashimara in 1985 where they completed 20 years on the MiG-21FL. They converted onto the Mirage 2000 at Gwalior on 1st January 1986, using them with great success during Operation Safed Sagar over Kargil in 1999. The Tigers were the first IAF unit to be presented with the President Standard on 18th October 1968 and in 2008 they celebrated their Platinum Jubilee.

Crest: Officially approved by King George VI in October 1942 consisting of a Tiger.

Motto: The original motto of 'Ittehad Men Shakti Hai / Strength Through War' was a mix of Urdu and Sanskrit, to symbolise the secular character of the IAF. It was changed after Independence to 'Ekta Mein Shakti / Strength in Unity.'

Battle Honours:
Indo-Pak Conflict 1965
Entire Operations
Air Offensive

Indo-Pak Conflict 1999
Operation Safed Sagar

◀ Pilot Officer Henry Sathyanathan, possibly at Juhu circa March 1942.

▼ 1 Squadron Spitfire Mk.VIII with squadron crest in September 1946.

1 Squadron

12 Squadrons, Patches, Heraldry & Artwork of the Indian Air Force: 1932-2016

1 Squadron

◀ Mystere IVA and pilot from the 1960's. The pilot probably is wearing a hand made patch attached with small metal poppers.

▶ Marshall of the IAF Arjan Singh at the 75th anniversary event at Gwalior in 2008. Wearing the special Platinum Jubilee, Tiger head, Tiger Mirage 2000 Delta and Tiger Head/M2000 patches. Singh commanded 1 squadron from September 1943 until August 1945. He was awarded the DFC in the field personally by Lord Mountbatten.

Flying Squadrons   13

1 Squadron

▲ 1 Squadron M2000 with logo on aircraft at Palam in 1997.

14   Squadrons, Patches, Heraldry & Artwork of the Indian Air Force: 1932-2016

1 Squadron

◀ Tiger squadron sign Gwalior 2003.

Flying Squadrons   15

2 SQUADRON
'WINGED ARROWS'

▼ 2 Squadron MiG-27 at Kalaikunda in 1999. The squadron crest having being blacked out as a result of Post Kargil, regulation change.

The second IAF squadron to be raised was number 2, some eight years after number 1 squadron. Raised at Peshawar on 1st April 1941 flying the Westland Wapiti they later operated from Miranshah and Kohat before re-equipping with the Hawker Audax followed later by the Westland Lysander in January 1942. In September 1942 they moved to Risalpur and converted onto the Hawker Hurricane I, moving to Ranchi in December 1942 for advanced fighter combat training. A brief sojourn saw them depart to Bhopal in January 1943 and later to Imphal in April 1943 where they supported the Chindit Campaign. In May 1943 they moved to Trichinapolly and then to Kanchrapara in November 1944 where they got the Hurricane IIB. They deployed to Mambur by December 1944 where they joined 4 and 9 squadrons for the commencement of the second Arakan Campaign. After the war in January 1946 they moved to Kohat in the North West Frontier Province (NWFP) and converted onto the Spitfire Mk.VIII and Harvard, then going to Poona for Tempest conversion on 5th February 1947. Disbandment followed in March 1948 before they were raised again at Palam on the 15th July 1951 with the Supermarine Spitfire Mk.XVIII and the NA Harvard. They joined the jet age in October 1953, converting onto the De Havilland Vampire FB52 at Halwara, later

16 ◉ Squadrons, Patches, Heraldry & Artwork of the Indian Air Force: 1932-2016

converting onto the Dassault Ouragon in May 1956 at Amritsar. Between December 1957 and March 1962 they operated out of Halwara, moving onto Ambala where they converted to the Gnat on 4th April 1962. In April 1965 they departed for Bareilly in Central India, before returning west during the September 1965 war with Pakistan. During this conflict they operated from Ambala with detachments at Halwara and Agra. During this time the squadron's aircraft were involved in combat air patrols, bomber escorts and fighter interception. The Winged Arrows continued at Ambala and during the 1971 War they maintained a detachment at Amritsar. Their primary role was air defence and escort missions on counter air strikes and by war end they had flown 279 sorties. After the war the squadron moved to Srinagar in February 1975, staying there until October 1979. Thence they moved to Kalaikunda where they continued to fly the Gnat until February 1983, converting to the Ajeet in November of the same year. The Winged Arrows were the last IAF unit to fly the Ajeet and passed their last airworthy example onto the IAF museum at Palam on 25th March 1991. They then converted onto the MiG-27 at Kalaikunda in April 1991 and flew this type until 2003. They re-equipped with the Su-30MKI in June 2009. Awarded the President Standard on 15th December 1979.

▲ 2 Squadron logo on a Gnat.

Crest: *An Arrow with a pair of wings with the number two superimposed in the centre of two concentric circles with the Ashoka on top.*

Motto: *'Amogh Lakshya / True To Aim.'*

Battle Honours:
Indo-Pak Conflict 1965
Entire Operations
Air Offensive

▲ 2 Squadron MiG-27 about to drop its chute at Kalaikunda.

2 Squadron

2 Squadron

▲ 2 Sqn Su-30MKI taxiing off the runway at RAF Coningsby whilst participating in Exercise Indradhanush 2015.

Flying Squadrons 19

2 Squadron

▲ One of four 2 Sqn Su-30MKI's deployed to RAF Coningsby for Exercise Indradhanush 2015.

▲ 2 Sqn aircrew march out to their aircraft for another sortie during Exercise Indradhanush 2015.

3 SQUADRON
'COBRAS'

The Cobras were formed at Peshawar on 1st October 1941 on the Hawker Audax and after work up, it's A flight was detached to Miranshah to perform policing duties over the NWFP being replaced in February 1942 by its B Flight. A detachment was sent to Hyderabad in Sind Province between May and September 1942 to carry actions operations against a local tribe. In September 1943 they moved to Risalpur and converted onto the Hawker Hurricane IIC. Advanced training was given at Phaphamau and at the SLAIS in Ranchi enabling them to be fully operational. In February 1944 they moved to Kohat in the NWFP and policing duties were performed against local tribesmen. In 1945 the Cobras moved East to take part in the Burma campaign initially from Bawli North and during their three month tour they completed 493 operational sorties. On April 18th 1945 they moved to St Thomas Mount near Madras, later moving onto Risalpur before going to Yelahanka on 28th December 1945 for conversion to the Spitfire Mk.VIII. After that they moved to Kolar in February 1946 and became the first IAF unit to commence conversion to the Tempest II in April 1946, receiving their aircraft in November and then moving to Poona in January 1947.

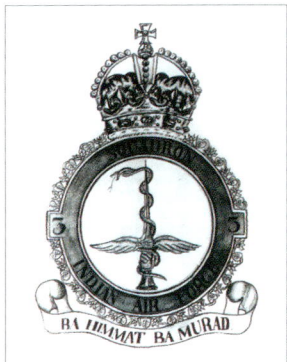

▲ WWII un-approved crest was later revised and approved in 1945.

▼ A Cobras MiG-21BIS taken in 2001 (Peter Steinemann).

Crest: The WWII crest consists of a winged dagger with a Cobra wrapped around it, together with a set of wings. Post Independence it was changed slightly and made up of four elements. The Dagger signifying the most common weapon of the North West Frontier Province, where the squadron was raised. The couped hand celebrates the role played by the squadron in holding the frontier. The Cobra signifies the aggressive fighting spirit of the squadron and finally the wings representing the flying aspect.

Motto: The original WWII motto was 'Ba Himmat Ba Murad / Fortune Favours the Brave' and this was changed in September 1954 to 'Lakshya Vedh / Destroy The Target With Precision'.

Battle Honours:

Indo-Pak Conflict 1965
A) Armoured Thrust
Chhamb-Jourian

B) Lahore Kasur Sector
Lahore Kasur

▲ Air Chief Marshall Dilbagh Singh in front of a 3 Squadron MiG-21BIS named in his honour.

During 1948 the squadron took part in Operation Polo over the State of Hyderabad. Here they provided reconnaissance and close air support to Indian Troops involved in the liberation of the territory which had elected to become part of Pakistan during the partition of India. In December 1952 they converted onto the Vampire FB52 at Ambala, later passing onto the Ouragon in February 1954 and then the Mystere IVA in May 1958 which corresponded with a move to Kalaikunda. In 1963 they moved west to Pathankot which was to be there home for the next eight years. September 1965 saw 3 squadron involved in operations on the

▼ 3 Squadron personnel in front of a squadron Mystere IVA.

22 Squadrons, Patches, Heraldry & Artwork of the Indian Air Force: 1932-2016

3 Squadron

western front. In 22 days the unit flew 290 missions consisting of counter air strikes against Pakistani Airfields, ground attacks against armour and troop concentrations and interdiction against infrastructure. The 1971 war saw them operating as one of the last two Mystere IV squadrons alongside 31 squadron at Hindon and on the eve of the conflict one flight of Mysteres moved to Sirsa with 31 squadron. The Sirsa Flight was tasked with close air support for the IA and in the first week completed several successful missions against railway infrastructure. By war end they had flown 76 hours of operations. Post war the squadron commenced their delayed conversion on to the MiG-21FL at Hindon in March 1972, followed by a move to Pathankot in December 1973 where they converted onto the MiG-21BIS in September 1980. They moved to Ambala in April 1997, where they have remained and converted onto the MiG-21UPG in July 2002. Awarded the President Standard on 18th March 1975.

▲ WWII era official crest as approved by King George VI.

Flying Squadrons　23

4 SQUADRON
"THE FIGHTING OORIALS"

The Oorials were raised at Peshawar on 1st February 1942 flying the Lysander. At that time local Afghan tribesman used to conduct fights using local mountain sheep known as Oorials, the animal having a reputation for being a ferocious fighter. So it was that the squadron adopted this animal as their emblem. The squadron moved onto Kohat before converting to the Hurricane IIC at Risalpur in June 1943. They continued to work up on the Hurricane IIC at Armada Road and Cox's Bazaar from where they commenced an operational tour against the Japanese in Burma. The role of the squadron was to provide close air support for the XIV Army and as that Army advanced through Burma, so did the squadron operating from various forward air landing grounds. The squadron took part in the Arakan offensive in December 1944, acting in direct support of land forces by attacking several Japanese strong points. In April 1945 the squadron was transferred back to Yelahanka for conversion onto the Spitfire Mk.VIII. By May 1945 they were operational on the new type and in August were selected to be part of the British Commonwealth Occupation forces in Japan. They received new equipment in the form of the Spitfire Mk.XIVe in December 1945 before setting off in HMS *Vengeance* on 8th April 1946

▼ Spitfire Mk.XIV's and pilots of 4 squadron at Yelahanka in March 1946 before setting of for Japan as part of British Commonwealth Occupation Force.

24 Squadrons, Patches, Heraldry & Artwork of the Indian Air Force: 1932-2016

via Singapore to Iwakuni in Japan. From there they moved to Miho from where they conducted maritime patrol missions and formation flying over large Japanese cities. In February 1947 they returned to Kanpur and were re-equipped later in October with the Tempest II, fulfilling the role of a training squadron. In September 1948 they moved from Kanpur to Gannavaram airstrip on the outskirts of Hyderabad in order to participate in Operation Bolo against the forces of the Nizam. The squadron strafed the airfields of Hakimpet and Warangal Town and aided IA forces in the capture of Suryapet. After the action they moved to Pune to resume its role as a training unit, from where pilots off the Spitfire course at Hakimpet joined for conversion training. They continued to fly the Tempest II until 1955, being the last squadron to do so, eventually converting onto the Vampire and moving to Adampur and then Halwara in 1956. In 1958 they moved to Ambala whereupon they took on the Ouragons from 8 squadron. They then moved to Palam and later moved east to Tezpur in 1960. In December 1961, the Oorials temporarily moved to Jamnager in order to participate in operations against the Portuguese enclaves of Goa, Daman and Diu. They flew several missions against Diu airfield

Crest: The squadron crest depicts an Oorial which is a wild sheep commonly found in the area of Peshawar where they were first raised. The emblem was adopted in December 1944 and officially sanctioned in July 1946 by King George VI. The squadron motto was written at the bottom of the crest and post Independence the Crown was replaced by the Ashoka on the top.

Motto: 'Maan Par Jan / Honour Unto Death'.

▼ Oorials' pilots in front of a squadron Ouragon.

Flying Squadrons 25

4 Squadron

▲ Flight Lieutenant Malik Nur Khan, then part of the 4 squadron detachment in Japan, later went on to command the Pakistan Air Force.

knocking out the runway and ATC with 500 lb bombs. The Indo-Pak conflict of 1965 saw them back at Tezpur from where they operated their single strike mission of the war on the 7th September against the airfield at Lal Munir Hat. In 1966 the Oorials gave up the Ouragon and became the fourth squadron to convert onto the MiG-21FL. By 1971 they were commanded by Wg Cdr. J.V. Gole and were operating from Guwahati for the duration of the Bangladesh Liberation War. They conducted counter air missions against the airfields of Kurmitola and Tezgoan commencing on 6th December, continuing with attacks against the same targets and additional missions in support of the Indian Army advance. The War end on the 17th December saw the unit having racked up 268 sorties with the loss of one aircraft. Post September 1971 they remained at Guwahati and moved to Bareilly in 1976 and Hashimara in 1979. Whilst back in Eastern Air Command they received the President Standard in a ceremony at Kalaikunda on 15th December 1979. In 1981 they moved back west to Pune airbase where they converted onto the MiG-21BIS, later moving to Uttarlai in 1985. In 2004 they converted onto the MiG-21UPG.

▲ 4 Squadron pilots on a Toofani during the 1960's.

▲ Air Marshall (Marshall of the IAF) Arjan Singh, outside the 4 Squadron HQ, 1960's.

▲ Two 4 squadron pilots in Japan wearing two versions of the earliest IAF patches.

26 Squadrons, Patches, Heraldry & Artwork of the Indian Air Force: 1932-2016

4 Squadron

▲ Group Captain Denzil Keelor (on the right), Commandant General of 4 Squadron in front of the squadron Standard.

▲ Pilots of 4 Squadron on a MiG-21FL.

▲ Group Captain Denzil Keelor inspecting the cockpit of a MiG-21FL.

Flying Squadrons 27

4 Squadron

▲ MiG-21BIS of 4 Squadron in the 1970's.

▲ 4 squadron mural at current homebase.   ▲ Oorials' operations complex with pilots in 2013.

28   Squadrons, Patches, Heraldry & Artwork of the Indian Air Force: 1932-2016

4 Squadron

▲ Oorials' pilots in front of mural circa 1970's.

▲ Post independence crest.

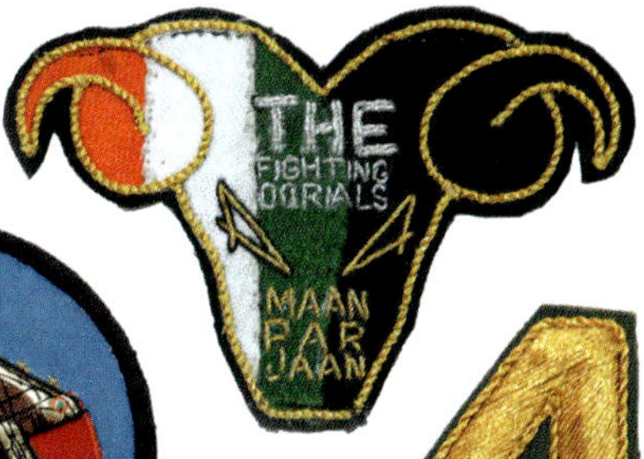

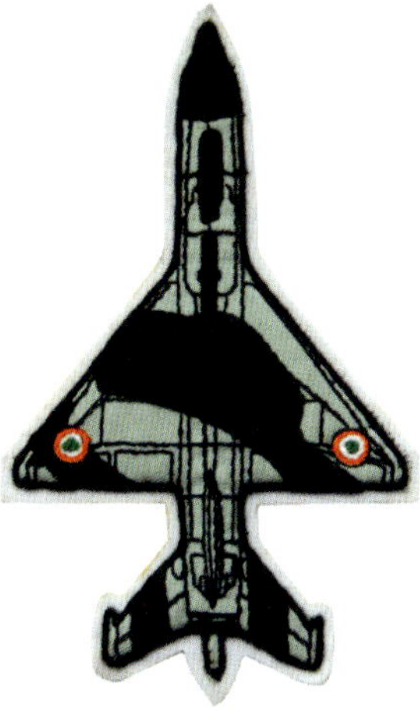

Flying Squadrons   29

5 SQUADRON
'TUSKERS'

▲ Official squadron crest on silk.

No squadron was raised pre WWII as the RAF already had a squadron with the same number operational in India. The Tuskers were raised on 2nd November 1948 at Agra with the B-24 Liberator becoming the IAF's first dedicated bomber squadron. On 1st May 1957 they converted onto the Canberra and continued with this type at Agra until 1981. During that time as the initial IAF Canberra unit they had acted as a conversion unit for other squadrons and had pioneered the type's development and operational expansion. For 14 months from October 1961 they had a successful United Nations stint in the Congo with 6 aircraft. During the 1965 War they flew over 300 missions consisting of counter air missions against several Pakistani Airfields and supported the Army with strikes against troops and armour concentrations. During the 1971 War they mounted the first strike mission against Pakistani airfields and once again flew missions in support of the IA, flying over 300 missions in 14 days. In August 1981 they moved to Ambala whereupon they converted onto the Jaguar IS. In July 1988 they undertook several reconnaissance missions over Sri Lanka during Operation Pawan which was supporting the IPKF. In 1997 they were the first IAF squadron to undertake air to air refuelling trials with a RAF VC-10. Awarded the President Standard on 9th April 1975.

▼ 5 Squadron B-24 in the 1950's.

▲ Canberra B(I)58 were in service with 5 Squadron between May 1957 and May 1981.

Crest: The crest of the squadron is a fully grown Elephant in a roundel, placed directly below the state emblem which is an adaptation from Sarnath Lion Capital of Emperor Ashoka. The mighty Tusker with a twisted tail is shown blowing its trumpet before the charge.

Motto: *Shakti Vijayete* / Strength is Victory.

Flying Squadrons 31

5 Squadron

▲ Wg Cdr Matheswaran, Commanding Officer of 5 Squadron in 1995.

32   Squadrons, Patches, Heraldry & Artwork of the Indian Air Force: 1932-2016

6 SQUADRON
'DRAGONS'

6 squadron were formed on 1st December 1942 at Trichinopoly on the Hurricane IIB and after training at 151 OTU, Risalpur, they moved to Bhopal in March 1943. From here they went to Cholavaram in Madras, Trichinopoly, Kaylan and Kolhapur and then in November they moved to Cox's Bazaar for operations over Burma. Operations started in November 1943 in support of XV Corps over the Arakan Front with their prime objective being tactical reconnaissance and offensive patrolling. Between 13th November 1943 and 28th February 1944 they achieved over 1000 operational sorties which was the highest recorded by any allied squadron in the 3rd Tactical Air Force. Such was their performance really appreciated by SEAC, that they were referred to as 'The Eyes of the 14th Army' and their commanding officer, Sqn Ldr Mehar Singh was awarded the DSO, becoming the only IAF Officer to receive this award. On the 15th April Flying Officer J.C. Verma shot down a Japanese Oscar which was the only confirmed aerial victory by the IAF in WWII. They moved to Buthidaung and flew their last operational sortie on 31st May 1944, withdrawing from theatre on 6th June and moving to Risalpur. In August 1944 they moved to Kohat and a flight was detached to Miranshah, where they flew air control duties over the NWFP. Conversion to the Spitfire Mk.VIII and Mk.XIV commenced in November 1945, later receiving the Spitfire PR.XI

▲ WWII Crest as approved by the RAF badge committee. The first version of a 6 squadron crest showed an Eagle on a fist.

▼ Jaguar IM lifts off from Pune in 2001.

in March 1946. Between April 1947 to May 1947 they moved to Karachi and re-equipped with the Dakota and upon Independence the entire squadron was ceded to Pakistan, with the remaining Indian personnel being integrated into 12 squadron. In February 1951 the squadron re-emerged at Pune in the maritime reconnaissance and air sea rescue role with B-24 Liberators. These lasted for 18 years and were supplemented in 1961 by nine Lockheed L-1049E Super Constellations that were surplus to Air India requirements. The induction of the Super Constellation enabled 6 squadron to commence transport support roles and the aircraft were widely used during the 1962 border war with China. In 1965 war they were tasked with maritime reconnaissance over the Arabian Sea, performed by Liberators operating off the coast from Okha to Cochin and the Super Constellations were used for transport, trooping and CASEVAC. The last Liberators were withdrawn at the end of 1968 and several were donated to overseas museums. War came again in 1971 and this time the Super Constellations were used in the MR role, flying a total of 386 hours over a period of 14 days. In January 1972 the squadron was part re-equipped with the Canberra B(I).58 enabling it to perform a maritime strike role and these were later joined by 5 Canberra TT418 aircraft enabling them to perform target towing duties for the various services. In the meantime the five remaining MR equipped Super Constellations were handed over to the Navy in November 1976 as that service assumed the role. This left 6 squadron with two converted L-1049G aircraft in the transport role and these soldiered on until being declared obsolete in September 1984. On 31st March 1987 at the HAL factory in Bangalore they received a unique variant of the Jaguar equipped for maritime strike. Initially the Jaguar IM equipped one flight of the squadron flying side by side with the Canberras until the latter were passed onto the Target Tug Flight at Agra in June 1992. The first six Jaguar IM's were supplemented by an additional batch and today the squadron continues to fly this sub type alongside examples of the Jaguar IS and IT. The squadron received the President Standard on 20th December 1980 and celebrated its 70th Anniversary in December 2012.

Crest: Two versions of the original crest from WWII are known to exist. The first one has an Eagle on a fist with the motto 'Tarshyo Arisht Naime' and the second one has an Eagle clutching a snake in its talons with the motto 'Knows No Fear'. Post Independence it was re-designed by Sqn Ldr Ian 'Locky' Loughran to reflect its maritime role. The design depicts a Sea Dragon with both flippers and wings, representing its allegiance to the sea and sky. The crest was approved by the President on 10th December 1955. This crest is highly unorthodox because of the way the Dragon is drawn facing right and if it were on a flag being 'marched', the Dragon would be 'marched' tail first. All crests have objects facing to the left for this purpose.

Motto: As described above the original motto was 'Tarkshyo Arisht Naime / Knows no fear' and this was replaced post independence by 'Sada Satark / Always Alert'.

◀ Original WWII Crest as approved by King George VI.

34　Squadrons, Patches, Heraldry & Artwork of the Indian Air Force: 1932-2016

6 Squadron

▲ Induction of the Canberra into 6 Squadron in January 1972. 6 Sqn Lockheed L1049E Super Constellation in the background

Flying Squadrons   35

6 Squadron

▲ The squadron complex at Pune in 1998.

▲ Pre 1999 squadron badge plus bars on Jaguar IM, 1998.

▼ Current Dragons complex complete with Sea Eagle missiles.

Squadrons, Patches, Heraldry & Artwork of the Indian Air Force: 1932-2016

7 SQUADRON
'BATTLE AXES'

The Battle Axes were raised on 1st December 1942 at Vizagapatnam flying the Vultee Vengeance. They moved to Kohat for conversion flying and later gunnery training and their first action was against tribals in the area of North Waziristan on 3rd December 1943. They moved to Gwalior, Kumbhigram and Phaphamau where they flew several bombing missions against Japanese ground targets. The unit moved onto Peshawar in November 1944 and converted onto the Hurricane IIC at 152 OTU. The unit were deployed to Sinthe in April 1945 for a tour in Burma and from here their task was tactical reconnaissance and photo reconnaissance as they advanced down the country with 33 Corps. In June 1945 they moved to Samungli and by August 1945 they were flying anti malarial missions at Lahore, their aircraft having been converted to spray. On 19th November 1945 they commenced conversion at Gwalior onto the Spitfire Mk.VIII and Mk.XIV. By December 1945, they were operating a mix of both types having 11 Hurricane IICs, three Hurricane IVs, two Spitfire VIIIs, seven Spitfire XIVs and a Harvard. In August 1946 they moved to Miranshah only with the Spitfire and Harvard complement before transitioning to the Tempest at Risalpur in April 1947. Following Indian Independence in 1947 the squadron became involved in the first war with Pakistan

▼ 7 Squadron Mirage 2000 at Palam in 1997.

Crest: *The current logo was approved in September 1960, though the squadron have been using the emblem for some time. The 'Farsha' or Battleaxe was the favourite weapon of the mythical Lord Parshurama. It had 4 cutting edges and two unfurled wings adorning it on each side. The symbolic '7' is attached to the shaft of the axe, The Battleaxe symbolises the offensive capability of the squadron.*

Motto: *'Shatrunjay / Vanquish the Enemy'.*

Battle Honours:

Indo-Pak Conflict 1999 Operation Safed Sagar

over Jammu and Kashmir. They had moved to Agra in August before deploying up to Amritsar from where they flew 121 hours of operations in November. From here they moved to Palam and completed another tour in J&K in February 1948, flying another 122 hours made up of 46 sorties. They returned to Palam before being deployed to Srinagar from where they flew 170 hours of ops in August 1948, followed by 160 hours of ops in October and finally 170 hours in December before a UN brokered ceasefire came into effect on 1st January 1949. Returning to Palam after the war, 7 squadron amalgamated with the Aircraft Testing Unit which was operating the first three Vampire F3s delivered to the IAF. In December 1949 the Tempests were retired and the unit received Spitfire XVIIIs and by April 1950 were operating a mix of Vampires, Spitfires and Harvards. In November 1950 they received two Vampire FB52s; later becoming fully equipped with 12 Vampires FB52s by August 1951, with the Spitfires being transferred to 2 squadron. They moved to Halwara in 1954 and then back to Palam in 1956, before converting to the Hunter at Ambala in January 1958. The start of the 1965 war saw the unit based at Halwara from where they flew 453 sorties, totalling 332 hours. Missions included CAP, Interdiction, ground attack and armed reconnaissance. It was an eventful war for the squadron as they claimed two F-86 shot down with the loss of six Hunters over the two week period. Post 1965 the unit moved onto Hindon and Bagdogra before being deployed back to Hindon in December 1971 War. They were involved in close air support missions, but later on completed several interdiction missions against infrastructure in West Pakistan losing three Hunters. Post war they moved back to Eastern Air Command at Bagdogra before converting onto the MiG-21MF at Chandigarh in November 1973. They moved to Pathankot in May 1975 before returning to Chandigarh, where in October 1981 they transferred their MFs to 108 squadron, receiving the MiG-21M in lieu. In 1985 the MiG-21Ms were given to 51 squadron and 7

▶ Hunter pilots from 7 squadron, 1960's.

38 Squadrons, Patches, Heraldry & Artwork of the Indian Air Force: 1932-2016

7 Squadron

MiG-21 pilots from 7 Squadron, 1970's.

squadron converted to the Mirage 2000. Since conversion onto the Mirage 2000, 7 squadron have taken part in the Sri Lankan Operations in 1987 and the Maldives Operations of 1988 when they escorted IAF transport aircraft. In 1999 they took a very active role in Operation Safed Sagar, the historic battle with Pakistan over the high terrain in Kargil. 7 squadron were tasked with the precision delivery of guided bombs, a task which was rushed into service by the squadron ahead of schedule. By war end they had completed 254 strike missions and dropped 156 bombs, eight of which were the Litening/Paveway II combination. They were awarded the President Standard on 20th December 1980.

Squadron badge on aircraft 1998.

7 Squadron Mirage pilots 1990's.

Flying Squadrons   39

7 Squadron

40 Squadrons, Patches, Heraldry & Artwork of the Indian Air Force: 1932-2016

7 Squadron

Flying Squadrons | 41

8 SQUADRON
'EIGHTH PURSOOTS'

World War II un-approved crest.

Su-30MKI of 8 Squadron 2012.

The Eighth Pursoot were raised at Trichinopoly on the 1st December 1942 flying the Vultee Vengeance. They moved to 152 OTU at Phaphamau where they perfected their dive bombing technique and formation flying. They then moved to Double Moorings near Chittagong in December 1943 from where they flew 1420 sorties, dropping 1,379,200 lbs of ordnance in 8 months before departing to Quetta in July 1944. They were originally slated to go to the Mosquito, but that type's unsuitability in the Indian Climate meant that the next type would be the Spitfire Mk.VIII, which they received in October 1944 at Armada Road. These were replaced by Spitfire Mk.V's and after work up they moved to George Airstrip near Chittagong from where they provided CAP over the landings of the 25th Infantry Division. They moved to Baigachi in May 1945 for ground firing practice and air defence duties and then onto Dum Dum in Bombay where their aircraft were handed over to the resident R&SU. In July 1945 they moved to Mingaladon upon where they received 14 Spitfire Mk.VIII and commenced operations against the Japanese. In late 1945 they started to receive the Spitfire Mk.XIV and in January 1946 they moved to Trichinopoly, then Kolar in June of the same year. They converted to the Tempest II in April 1947 at Poona. After a short stay at Poona they commenced Jammu and Kashmir operations from Palam on 31st December 1947. Post war they remained at Palam where they converted onto the Vampire FB52 on 30th August 1951. They moved to Ambala in September 1953 to begin conversion onto the Ouragon which commenced on 1st November of the same year. In November 1957 they moved eastwards to Kalaikunda where upon they changed to the Mystere IV, moving back to Palam in 1962 and then onto Adampur where they stayed until November 1965. During the 1965 War they flew counter air missions against Pakistani Airfields including Sargodha and Bhagtanweala. They moved to Ambala in November 1965 where they converted onto the MiG-21FL on 17th February 1969. From Ambala they moved to Pune on 18th January 1971 and during the 1971 War moved to Bagdogra in the East where they were held in reserve. Moving back to Pune, the move to Bagdogra was made permanent in April 1989 after a two year spell at Hashimara. They ceased to operate the MiG-21FL in 2006, becoming numberplated before resurrection as the fourth Su-30MKI squadron in 2008. They were awarded the President Standard on 5th March 1984.

Crest: *Approved by the President on 10th September 1955. The WWII crest consisted of Leopard super imposed over a map of pre-partition India, together with the Latin motto 'Coelum Est Nostra /Heaven is ours'. Later in WWII the title 'Eight Pursoot' is believed to have been adopted whist the squadron was at Mingaladon. Here the ATC staff was predominantly of American origin and they referred to their squadrons as 'Pursuit'. Jokingly the pilots of 8 squadron started to call themselves the 'Eight Pursuit', changing it to the Eighth 'Pursoot'. Later the original WWII badge was replaced by an American Condor over the Star of India.*

Motto: *Post Independence the motto was changed to 'Suraksha Va Akraman / Offense is Defence'.*

◀ Squadron badge on MiG-21FL in 1998.

▶ Air Marshall Sir Gerald Gibbs, CBE, CIE, MC & Bar deplaning from an 8 squadron Vampire. Gibbs relinquished command of the IAF in 1954, being the last British Commander in Chief.

Flying Squadrons   43

8 Squadron

▲ Variation on the Squadron badge on MiG-21FL in 1998.

44 Squadrons, Patches, Heraldry & Artwork of the Indian Air Force: 1932-2016

9 SQUADRON
"WOLFPACK"

The squadron was raised on 13th November 1943 at 151 OTU, Risalpur. Next they went to 307 MU at Lahore to collect their Hurricane IIB's and moved to Bhopal on 7th January 1944 for a final work up. They then went to Kulaura near Sylhet on 29th March 1944 to support other IAF squadrons in the relief of Imphal. They were tasked with escorting Dakotas and flying patrols over the Imphal Valley and in May moved to Singerbill to sit out the monsoon. In July 1944 they commenced operations in support of XV Corps, consisting of attacks against river shipping and communications around Akyab. In January 1945 the supported beach landings at the tip of the Maebon Peninsular and in February supported the operations along the Arakan Coast. Later that year they supported the amphibious landings by the East African Division at Ramree Island. On 14th April 1945 they moved to the SLIAS at Ranchi where they were to convert to the Spitfire Mk.VIII, which they started to receive in May. In October 1945 they moved to Baigachi, then Hmwabi and then Willingdon in January 1946. They commenced conversion to the Spitfire Mk.XIV and by the end of March 1946 all Spitfire Mk.VIII's had been retired. In January 1947 they moved to Bhopal and they were selected to be handed over to Pakistan. By April

▼ MiG-27 of 9 Squadron just after Kargil operations in 1999.

Crest: *The original WWII unit was known as the 'Dragons' and this came about because during their time in Burma, they adopted the Burmese Chinte, which is a mythical Dragon that guards their temples. Later they became known as the 'Wolfpack.*

Motto: *'Sahase Wasati Jayashrih / In Courage Resides Victory'.*

Battle Honours:

Indo-Pak Conflict 1999
Operation Safed Sagar

all aircraft had been flown to 320 MU at Karachi or the SFTS at Ambala. On the 3rd May 1947 they moved to Peshawar to convert onto the Tempest, taking over the aircraft of 5 squadron, RAF. The squadron stood down as an IAF unit on 14th August 1947 and all Indian personnel were repatriated. They were stood up on 16th March 1964 on the Gnat at Ambala and during the 1965 War with Pakistan they maintained CAP's over Ambala, Halwara and Adampur. On the 19th September 1965, whilst on an escort mission, Flt Lt V.K. Kapila shot down a PAF F-86 over the Chawinda-Pasrur Sector, earning himself the VrC. In 1966 the squadron left for Halwara and flew CAP's from there and Amritsar. They became the first squadron to stand up on the improved HAL Ajeet in March 1978, acting initially as the Ajeet Handling Flight, due to aircraft delivery problems. They became fully operational on the type by January 1980 and they soon proved their worth by winning the IAF gunnery meet in 1981. They converted onto the MiG-27 at Adampur, where they remained until 2001. During that time they took part in Operation Safed Sagar over Kargil 1999. They were numberplated in 2002, resurrecting in 2004 as the third Mirage 2000 squadron. They were awarded the President Standard on 11th December 1984 at Palam.

▼ Log book entry from David Bouche circa 1945 during Burma operations, confirming that 9 squadron was originally referred to as 'The Dragon Squadron'.

9 Squadron

9 squadron Gnat era 1960's.

Patches & Insignia of the Indian Air Force 47

9 Squadron

48 Squadrons, Patches, Heraldry & Artwork of the Indian Air Force: 1932-2016

10 SQUADRON
'DAGGERS'

The Winged Daggers were raised in Lahore under the command of Battle of Britain pilot, Squadron Leader Bob Doe on 20th February 1944. Their initial equipment was the Hurricane IIC and after work up they moved to Risalpur in May 1944 before proceeding to an armament course at Amarda Road in July. In November 1944 they were given an air to ground role with their Hurri-Bombers and moved to Ramu in the Arakan for operations. The third Arakan Campaign kicked off in December and the squadron commenced operations from Ramu on 23rd December. Through the month of January they gave support to the West African Division operating from the advance airstrip at Paukpingwin. Operations continued through February with their base moving to Akyab, then Bawli Bazar and later Kyaukpyu in March. In April 1945 they moved to Yelahanka as they were earmarked for conversion to the Spitfire Mk.VIII which they received in July, returning back to Burma via Trichinopoly for their base at Hmawbi. They remained in Burma till 15th February 1946 before returning to India at Baigachi and then Barrackpore in June 1946. The conversion to the Tempest commenced at Chakeri in May 1947 and they moved onto Ambala in November 1947. They saw operational service during the Jammu & Kashmir war between November 1947 and October 1948, operating from forward locations of Amritsar, Jammu and Srinagar. Their prime role being ground attack in support of advancing

▲ Commanding Officers of 10 Squadron from inception. Noteworthy is Battle of Britain Pilot, Wg Cdr Bob Doe DFC, their first c/o.

▼ MiG-27M of 10 squadron at Jodhpur in 1998.

Flying Squadrons

Indian Army armoured formations. After the conflict they moved to various locations over a short period of time including airfields in the Punjab and Rajasthan, moving to Calcutta in 1951 and Halwara in April 1952. They moved to Palam in December 1953 where they remained until April 1964. Whilst at Palam they first transitioned to the Vampire FB52 in December 1953 and then the night fighting Vampire NF54 in August 1954. In April 1964, whilst at Palam the squadron was numberplated and their ageing Vampire NF54's retired, later resurrecting at Jamnager in April 1967 with the HF-24 Marut. In May 1969 they moved to Pune and later to Jodhpur in December 1970. At the start of the 1971 tensions they moved a detachment of aircraft to the forward operating location of Uttarlai from where they carried out tactical reconnaissance, interdiction and ground attack missions. In May 1975 they took on the role of the type training squadron for the Marut, which they held until August 1980 when they handed over their aircraft in preparation to receive the MiG-23BN. They remained in suspended animation whilst pilots and ground crews went to Russia for training, re-surfacing in January 1981 after taking delivery of the first of the Russian swing wing aircraft at Nasik. They remained at Jodhpur with the MiG-23BN until they converted onto HAL manufactured MiG-27's in December 1993. They converted to the MiG-27UPG in 2008. Awarded the President Standard on 18th March 1985.

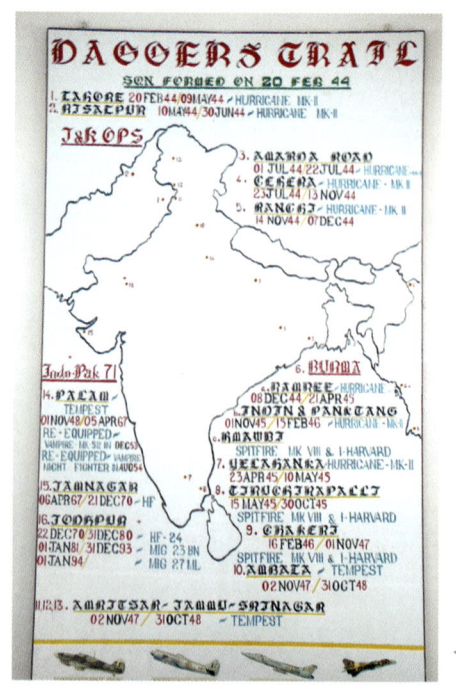

Crest: The existing logo of the squadron has been in use since the 1940's and was officially approved by the President of India in December 1955. The combination of the Dagger and Wings is designed to include the squadron number in Roman numeral portraying the unit's lethal intent of operations in the third dimension.

Motto: 'Yudhay Krutnischay / Into War With Determination'

Battle Honours:

Jammu & Kashmir
Operation 1947/48
Operations against raiders,
Defence of Srinagar Valley

Srinagar Valley
Defence of Srinagar Valley

◀ 10 Squadron theatre of operations.

50   Squadrons, Patches, Heraldry & Artwork of the Indian Air Force: 1932-2016

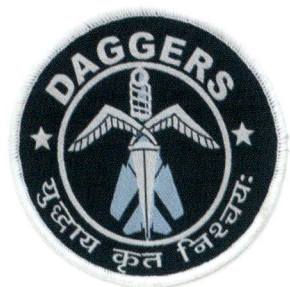

10 Squadron

▲ 10 Squadron badge on a preserved MiG-23BN at Halwara.

▲ 10 Squadron Badge on a MiG-27 at Jodhpur in 1998.

▶ 10 squadron MiG-23BN showing off its offensive capabilities.

Flying Squadrons 51

10 Squadron

▲ 10 Squadron MiG-27UPG landing at Jodhpur during Exercise Iron Fist in 2013.

52   Squadrons, Patches, Heraldry & Artwork of the Indian Air Force: 1932-2016

10 Squadron

▲ 10 Squadron MiG-27UPG at Jodhpur in 2013.

Flying Squadrons

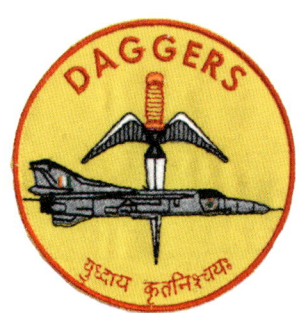

11 SQUADRON
'RHINOS'

No IAF squadron was raised pre war as the RAF had an 11 squadron active in India at the time. On 11th November 1951, the squadron was raised at Barrackpore with a compliment of ten Dakota aircraft. In February 1961 they moved to Jorhat with other moves to Barrackpore and Bakshi Ka Talab. In this period the flew missions in the 1962 and 1965 wars and supported IA Operations in the NEFA. They participated in the Tangail Para drop over East Pakistan on 11th December 1971 when 22 Dakotas were used to drop 423 paratroopers. In April 1979 the Avro 748 was inducted into the squadron and for a time both aircraft were operated until the Dakota was retired in July 1980. In 1987 they were involved in Operation Pawan, which was the Indian Peace Keeping Mission to Sri Lanka. Here they performed reconnaissance, casualty evacuation and communications duties for the entire period. In January 1996 they moved to Sulur and converted onto the Antonov 32 which enabled them to operate the courier service to Car Nicobar in the Andaman Islands, which they had instigated whilst at Barrackpore in 1956. They moved to Baroda in March 2000 where upon they converted back to the HS-748. They were awarded the President Standard on 18th March 1985.

Crest: : The squadron crest and motto were chosen when they moved to Jorhat in 1961. The Rhino was chosen as it is well known for its courage and strength and the one horned variety being a popular resident of the nearby Kaziranga sanctuary.

Motto: The motto is the Sanskrit 'Vishwambarah Prandah / Supporters Of The Universe'

54 Squadrons, Patches, Heraldry & Artwork of the Indian Air Force: 1932-2016

12 SQUADRON
'STRIKING YAKS'

The IAF's first transport squadron was raised with Spitfire Mk.VIII at Kohat on 1st December 1945, pending availability of suitable transport aircraft. In January 1946 they moved to Risalpur and received the Oxford for twin training conversion. In May 1946 the Spitfires left the unit and they moved home to Bhopal to receive the Dakota, arriving there on 1st June 1946. The squadron's finest hour occurred in October 1947, when during the first Indo-Pak War over Kashmir their prompt action by airlifting in troops and supplies, prevented Srinagar from falling into enemy hands. In 1954 the squadron were selected to induct the first C-119's in the IAF with their Dakotas lasting until 1958 when they were passed to 43 Squadron at Barrackpore. In October 1962, during the Sino-Indian War they were kept busy flying in supplies for the IA into Awantipur, Chosul and Thoise. A detachment of 12 squadron operated from Guwahati in support of troops in the NEFA and airlifted an artillery regiment to Tezpur. During the Indo-Pak Wars of 1965 and 1971 they performed a logistical air bridge to all parts of Western Air Command. The squadron soldiered on with the C-119 until the Antonov 32 replaced it in July 1984 becoming the first squadron to operate the type in the IAF. They were awarded the President's Standard at Agra on 12th March 1971.

Crest: The crest consists of a Yak.

Motto: 'Amit Vikram / Unlimited Valour'.

▲ 12 Squadron logo on an An-32 in the 1990's.

◀ Yaks' pilots in front of their C-119.

Flying Squadrons 55

14 SQUADRON
'BULLS'

The squadron was raised on 15th August 1951 on the Spitfire Mk.XVIII and during April 1952 they moved to Barrackpore where they would stay for five years. The squadron took part in Operation Mop, against tribesmen in the NEFA during November and December 1953 from a detachment at Jorhat. The Bulls traded in their Spitfires in September 1957 and moved to Halwara in order to convert onto the Vampire FB52. After conversion in 1958 they moved to Adampur, however severe monsoon flooding in 1959 forced the unit out to Palam and then Ambala where they converted onto the Hunter F56. Conversion training commenced on 12th October 1959 and after becoming operational they detached to Halwara during the Chinese crisis of November 1962, before moving to their permanent home for the next 17 years at Kalaikunda. During the 1965 war with Pakistan they were under the command of Wg Cdr Dennis La Fontaine, and tasked with air defence and fighter sweeps over East Pakistan. On 7th September 1965 an incoming raid by Sabres of 14 squadron, PAF were intercepted by Hunters of 14 squadron, IAF. In the ensuing battle Flight Lt Alfred Cooke shot down one of the Sabres and seriously damaged another, which crashed upon its return to Tezgaon. During the 1971 war a detachment operated from Dum Dum Airport in Calcutta from where they CAP's and counter air strikes against the airfields of Tezgaon and Chittagong. During one mission on the 4th December the squadron c/o, Wg Cdr R. Sundaresan shot down a PAF F-86, whilst on his third mission of the day. Later they commenced a series of ground attack missions against strategic targets before deploying to the former PAF base at Jessore in East Pakistan, later returning to Kalaikunda

56 Squadrons, Patches, Heraldry & Artwork of the Indian Air Force: 1932-2016

Crest: *The squadron crest was adopted in August 1956 and consists of a fighting bull which is taken from a 6th or 7th century wall painting found in the Ajanta Caves in Maharashtra. The official squadron crest was approved by AVM Arjan Singh DFC on 4th May 1962.*

on 21st December 1971. A total of 229 sorties were flown over the two week period. Over the next few years the squadron offered type training on the Hunter continuing on type until July 1979 when their aircraft were passed onto the OCU, which became the Hunter Operational Flying Training Unit. The Bulls were selected to be the first squadron on the Jaguar at Ambala and the first pilots were sent to the UK for training in February 1979. The first of 18 ex RAF aircraft arrived at Ambala on 29th July 1979. They were declared operational on the Jaguar in September 1980 and took on the role of training Jaguar Pilots for other squadrons. The Bulls were honoured with the presentation of the President Standard on 11th November 1994 at Ambala. During Operation Safed Sagar the IAF's Kargil operations in 1999 they participated in photo reconnaissance missions over enemy troop positions. In 2004 they deployed to Alaska to participate in a Cope Thunder exercise at Eielson AFB.

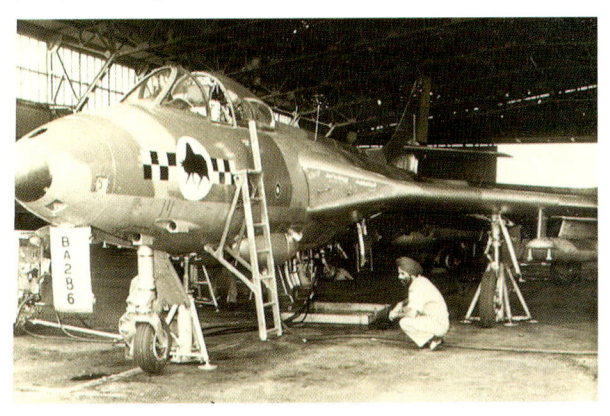

Motto: *'Balam Jayay / Victory in Power'. This signifies the offensive capability of a deep penetration strike squadron.*

▲ 14 Squadron Hunter F56.

Flying Squadrons   57

15 SQUADRON
'FLYING LANCES'

The Flying Lances were raised at Ambala on 20th August 1951 flying the Spitfire Mk.XVIII. However its life was short lived as it was re-numbered as 1 squadron on 25th January 1953. The squadron was resurrected on 21st November 1964 with the Folland Gnat. During the 1965 War it moved from Ambala to Agra for the duration where it flew air defence missions, later loaning out eight of its aircraft to bolster other Gnat squadrons on the frontline. Post war the unit continued to operate the Gnat having moved onto Kalaikunda, then Mumbai, Bagdogra and Ambala before moving back to Bagdogra in time for the 1971 War. During this conflict the unit flew 26 combat air patrol missions and nine strike missions from home base. They also operated detachments at Hashimara from where they flew more combat air patrols and deep penetration strikes and also kept a two aircraft detachment running at Argatala. The final total being over 300 combat missions in 14 days. In 1975 they moved to Pune where they converted onto the MiG-21BIS, remaining there until they moved to Bhuj in 1981. Here their role was that of air defence, close air support and fighter reconnaissance. In 1995 they took on the additional task of training, being part of the MOFT syllabus. They moved from Bhuj in 2001 following the earthquake which wrecked the base. They operated from Nal/Bikaner in Rajasthan, until they were numberplated in 2009. Awarded the President Standard on 26th October 1995. They have since converted to the Su-30MKI.

▲ 15 Squadron MiG-21BIS at Jodhpur in 1998.

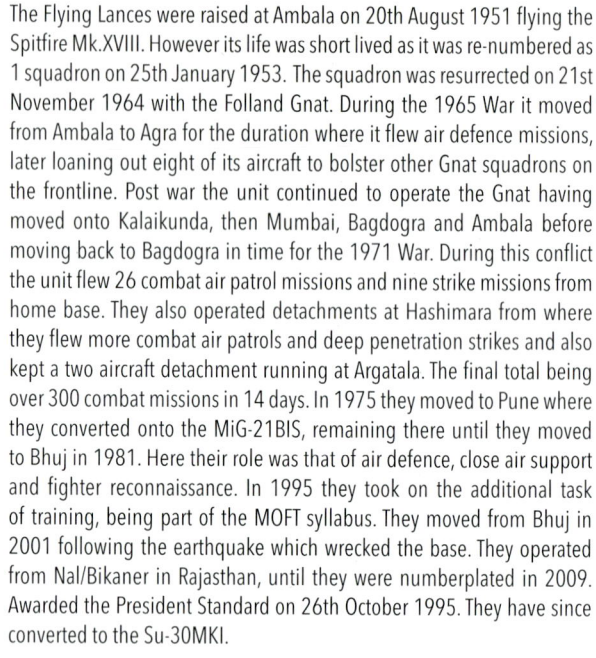

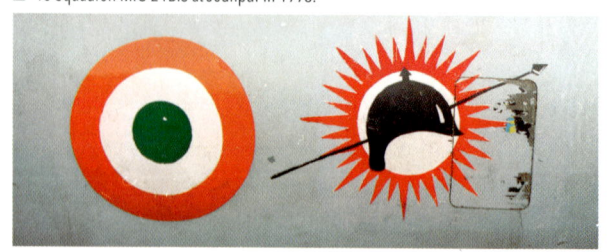

▲ Close up of the 15 Squadron logo. Signs on the inspection panel of the previous MOFTU ownership.

58   Squadrons, Patches, Heraldry & Artwork of the Indian Air Force: 1932-2016

Crest: *A spear and helmet of the Suryavanshi Sect of the Rajputs over an image of the sun. The spear head of the Rajputs was cavalry and therefore the crest depicts the lance and helmet. The sun signifies the nobility and purity of the Rajputs. The wings of the lance symbolise the swiftness and mobility of their aerial aspect.*

Motto: *'Nihantavya Shatrava / Annihilation Of The Enemy.'*

Flying Squadrons

16 SQUADRON
'BLACK COBRAS'

The Cobras were formed at Pune in 1950 with a mix of Spitfires and Tempest II's. In 1954 they converted onto the B-24 Liberator and took on the role of training bomber crews. In 1957 the re-equipped with the Canberra B(I)58 and they took part in bombing operations during Operation Vijay against the Portuguese airfield of Dabolim in Goa. They left Pune in 1962 for Kalaikunda in the east from where they operated initially in the counter air role against targets in East Pakistan during the 1965 war, under the command of Wg Cdr Peter Wilson. After suffering badly during an air strike at Kalaikunda airfield they re-grouped and moved to operations in the west where they flew strike missions against Sargodha Airfield and completed a successful strike mission against the heavily defended radar station at Badin. After the war the squadron moved to Gorakhpur and in 1971 took part in operations against East and West Pakistan. On November 13th 1976 they received the President Standard and converted onto the Jaguar in 1986.

▼ 16 Squadron Jaguar IS taxies at Jodhpur in 1998.

Squadrons, Patches, Heraldry & Artwork of the Indian Air Force: 1932-2016

▲ RAAF Crew zaps a 16 Squadron Canberra at Kalaikunda in 1963, during the air defence exercise 'Shiksha'.

Crest: The squadron Crest is a Black Cobra in an aggressive posture.

Motto: 'Prahardyot / Ready to Strike'.

Battle Honours:

Indo-Pak Conflict 1965
Entire Operations
Air Defence

Flying Squadrons   61

16 Squadron

▲ 16 Squadron Standard.

▲ 16 Squadron logo on Jaguar IS.

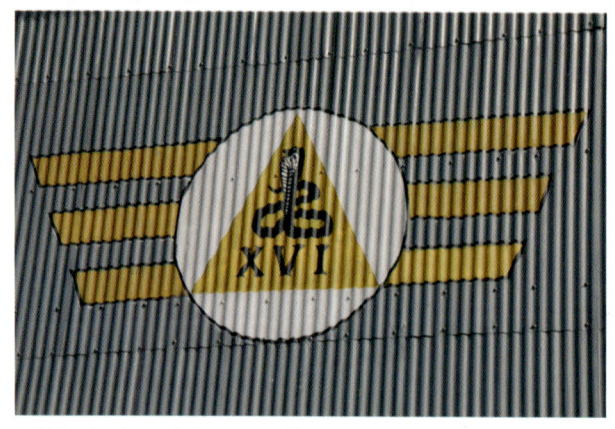

▲ 16 Squadron logo on the hangar at Gorakhpur.

17 SQUADRON
'GOLDEN ARROWS'

The squadron was raised on 1st October 1951 at Ambala on the Harvard. They moved to Adampur on 5th May 1952 and were allocated the task of Tactical Reconnaissance, moving back to Ambala in December 1952. They moved back to Adampur in December 1953, whereupon they started conversion onto the Vampire FB52, which was completed in November 1955. In August 1957, 17 squadron were selected to be the first Hunter squadron and the nucleus of pilots left for training in the UK. They stood up at Ambala with the Hunter in January 1958 and formed an aerobatic team to take part in the Republic Day flypast of 1958. The squadron moved to Pune on 3rd December 1958 and during the 1961 action to reclaim the former Portuguese colonies of Goa, Damman and Diu, six aircraft were deployed to Ambre from where they attacked the Bambolim wireless station near Goa with rocket projectiles. The balance of the unit mounted a combat air patrol from Pune over their locale which included the city of Mumbai. On 18th November 1962, they moved East to be based at Jorhat and during the 1965 war they flew CAP missions from there and Tezpur. By the time the 1971 War came around they were operating from Hashimara, with a 5 aircraft detachment at Kumbhigram and on the first day of the conflict carried out numerous close air support and counter air missions against targets in East Pakistan, including the airfields at Tezgaon and Kurmitola. In December 1974 they moved to Halwara in preparation for conversion on the MiG-21M, which they received in March 1975. In February 1982 they moved to Bathinda and on 18th May 1999 deployed to Srinagar to participate in the Kargil war. The main role of the squadron was fighter reconnaissance and they performed their first missions over the combat area on 21st May. Later during the conflict the squadron performed several bombing missions before the cessation of flying activities on 12th July 1999. They returned to Bathinda which continued to be their home until being numberplated in September 2011 after celebrating their Diamond Jubilee. They were awarded the President Standard on 8th November 1988.

Crest: *A stretched bow with golden arrow pointing heavenwards.*

Motto: *'Udayam Ajasram / Ever Rising Skywards'.*
Also known as the 'FR Pioneers'

Battle Honours:
Indo-Pak Conflict 1999
Operation Safed Sagar

Flying Squadrons 63

18 SQUADRON
'FLYING BULLETS'

Crest: The crest depicts a bullet with wings, ahead of which is a shock wave indicating supersonic flight.

Motto: 'Theevra Aur Nirbhay / Swift and Fearless'.

Battle Honours:
Indo-Pak Conflict 1971
Entire Operation
Air Defence

The squadron was formed on 15th April 1965 at Ambala with the Gnat and remained there until August 1971 when a detachment of four aircraft from the unit moved to Srinagar from where it participated during the 1971 War. During this conflict the prime role of the squadron was to defend the Kashmir Valley from Srinagar. Missions initially included strafing runs and escorting Vampires on bombing runs. Some dog fighting with PAF Sabres took place on the 7th December and on the 14th December Flying Officer Sekhon posthumously received India's highest gallantry award, the Param Vir Chakra for bravery in attacking a formation of PAF Sabres that were attacking Srinagar Airfield. During the engagement Sekhon and Flight Lt Ghuman got airborne with bombs dropping around them which later affected the ground controller's ability to vector in the defenders against the attackers. Sekhon made contact with the Sabres and proceeded to shoot one down from where upon he moved onto another pair of aircraft. At this point whilst engaging a second Sabre he took hits from another enemy aircraft which disabled his aircraft forcing him to eject. Unfortunately the parachute did not deploy owing to insufficient height and Sekhon died. After the conflict the detachment moved back to Ambala and then they moved to Srinagar in February 1975 where they converted onto the Ajeet in 1980. In 1985 they transferred to Sulur, then Bagdogra in February 1988 and then Hindon in May 1989, where it converted onto the MiG-27. In April 1996 it moved to Kalaikunda and took on the target tug role, converting three aircraft to accept banner towing. Awarded the President Standard on 28th November 2015 and numberplated in April 2016.

64   Squadrons, Patches, Heraldry & Artwork of the Indian Air Force: 1932-2016

18 Squadron

Flying Squadrons 65

19 SQUADRON

The squadron was raised on 1st August 1960 with the C-119 Packet. They later operated from Pathankot and Srinagar. They converted onto the An-32 and during Operation Pawan in Sri Lanka during July 1987, were busy in airlifting supplies for the Indian Army. They were numberplated at Tambaram in 1998.

Crest: *A hand holding grain superimposed over a mountain range.*

Motto: *'Kodati Mara Samarthanam / Nothing Is Difficult For The Capable.'*

▲ Preserved C-119 at Palam, showing the 19 Squadron logo at bottom right.

▲ 19 Squadron personnel and aircraft in the 1960's.

Squadrons, Patches, Heraldry & Artwork of the Indian Air Force: 1932-2016

20 SQUADRON
'LIGHTNINGS'

The Lightnings were formed at Halwara on 1st June 1956 and were initially equipped with the Vampire FB52. In 1959 the squadron re-equipped with the Hunter F56 at Ambala, before moving to Palam in 1960. During the 1965 war they operated from Hindon and maintained a detachment from Halwara. They commenced operations on the 8th September with close air support and interdiction missions, continuing until the 22nd of the same month. They lost two aircraft during the campaign. Post 1965 the squadron remained at Hindon and later in July 1971 took up residence at Pathankot with the Hunter F56A. They performed counter air, interdiction and close air support during the 1971 war, starting with attacks against PAF airfields on 4th December 1971. During the first four days of the war they flew 121 sorties and claimed several aircraft destroyed on the ground for the loss of two Hunters. In May 1975 they moved to Hindon, followed in 1981 by a move east to Hashimara. where the squadron was re-christened as The Thunderbolts and became the first formation aerobatic team of the

▼ 20 Squadron Su-30MKI during Aero India at Yelahanka.

Flying Squadrons 67

IAF. The squadron performed over 70 displays in a seven year period until the team was disbanded. The squadron were renamed the Lightnings and moved to Kalaikunda during May 1990. From here they took on the role of an operational conversion unit and continued with the Hunter until June 1996, when the type was retired after 37 years continuous service with the squadron. They converted to the MiG-21FL in the training role and moved to Chabua in February 1996 until numberplating in December 1997. The squadron was resurrected on the 20th May 2002 on the Su-30MKI after a nucleus of 8 pilots had returned from pilot training in Russia. On 27th July 2004 they inducted the MiG-21UPG and for a period of nine months operated the two aircraft side by side developing tactics that would lead to the full exploitation of both types. Today they operate from Pune and apart from their offensive role, offer training as the Su-30 operational

Crest: Three bars of lightning in conjunction with a Himalayan Eagle.

Motto: 'Like Lightning We Strike", which was later changed to 'Vegvankutobhayah / Fast & Furious'.

Battle Honours:

Indo-Pak Conflict 1971
A) Air Offensive West Pakistan
Air Offensive

B) Pakistani Offensive (J&K sector)
Air Defence

▼ Hunter T7 of 20 Squadron in the 1970's.

▲ Wg Cdr P.S. Brar, c/o of 20 Squadron and Team Leader of the Thunderbolts, 1982.

▼ Hunter F56 with 20 Squadron logo.

68   Squadrons, Patches, Heraldry & Artwork of the Indian Air Force: 1932-2016

conversion unit, a role they commenced in 2005. They were awarded the President Standard on 10th March 1992 and celebrated their Golden Anniversary on the 31st May 2006 at Pune.

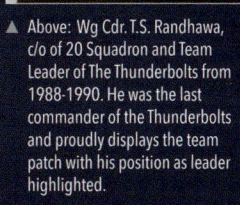

THE THUNDERBOLTS

Above: Wg Cdr. T.S. Randhawa, c/o of 20 Squadron and Team Leader of The Thunderbolts from 1988-1990. He was the last commander of the Thunderbolts and proudly displays the team patch with his position as leader highlighted.

Top: Thunderbolts' Pilot in crew room.

Flying Squadrons 69

21 SQUADRON
'ANKUSH'

The unit was raised at Ambala on 16th October 1965 and initially flew with Gnats loaned from other squadrons until receiving their compliment in May 1966. After work up they moved out to Gorakhpur and then Kalaikunda, which was to be there home for the next seven years. Although given a ground attack role, the 1971 War saw the unit divided up and providing combat air patrols over Uttarlai in the South West Sector and Amritsar in the Western sector, before moving to Ahmedabad. The unit flew 109 air defence sorties during the war and in that period only had one encounter with the enemy when the airfield at Uttarlai was attacked by two F-104s, which evaded two Gnats on a combat air patrol. Post war they took on the Gnat training role and moved to Bakshi Ke Talab in 1975 before relinquishing their aircraft. In 1976 they moved to Pune to begin conversion onto the MiG-21BIS, being the first squadron to do so. The initial cadre of pilots and technicians consisted of officers trained on the MiG-21 in the Soviet Union and after work up the unit was given the role of conversion training for other squadrons going onto the type. By the end of the first year, 21 squadron was fully operational having completed live weapons firing and had also converted 46 pilots for other squadrons onto the MiG-21. In 1986 the unit moved onto Jamnager remaining there until 1988 before going onto Chandigarh. They converted to the MiG-21UPG in 2003 and received the President Standard in March 2015.

Crest: *The Ankush is a device used by the Mahouts. (Elephant Handlers).*

Motto: *'Siddhivasti Saha Se / Success Lies In Courage'.*

22 SQUADRON
'SWIFTS'

Raised with Gnat at Bareilly on 15th October 1966, the squadron moved to Kalaikunda in September 1968 and prior to the 1971 war with Pakistan, operated a detachment at Dum Dum Civil Airport in Calcutta. From here they commenced air defence missions starting in September and during one of these on 22nd November 1971 they engaged four PAF sabres that had entered Indian Airspace over the Boyra Salient, resulting in the shooting down of three aircraft. The successful pilots, F/O Lazarus, P/O Ganapathy and P/O Massey were awarded the VrC for their feat. During the ensuing war 22 squadron operated in the air defence role, the ground attack role and gave close air support to the advancing Indian Army around Jessore. Counter air strikes were also conducted against the airfields at Brisal and Ishurdi. The unit re-equipped with the locally produced Ajeet in March 1982 and moved to Hashimara in February 1990, relinquishing their diminutive aircraft in favour of the MiG-27M from April 1990 onwards. Awarded the President Standard on 28th November 2015.

Crest: A Swift, a bird that has wings like modern fighter aircraft which are designed for high speed and manoeuvrability. Also the Swift has a keen sense of sight which enables it to spot and intercept its prey from a great distance. The crest was approved by the President of India on 20th December 1985. Previously they had been known as 'the Sabre Slayers', a title that apparently was never officially recognised.

Motto: Sahase Vijayate / Courage Triumphs'.

Battle Honours:

Indo-Pak Conflict 1971
Air Offensive for Liberation of Bangladesh
Air Offensive

Flying Squadrons

23 SQUADRON
'PANTHERS'

Formed at Poona on 1st October 1956 with the Vampire FB52, 23 squadron later went onto to become the first Gnat squadron in the IAF in May 1960, when they inherited several aircraft from the Gnat Handling Unit at Ambala. During the 1965 war they were forward deployed to Pathankot from where they provided top cover and succeeded in shooting down three PAF F-86s. The first of these on the 3rd September followed a trap set by the IAF to lure PAF fighters into attacking two Mystere IV bombers. Unbeknown to the attacking F-86s and F-104s, a formation of 23 squadron Gnats were waiting to pounce and so Sqn Ldr Trevor Keelor had the honour of achieving the IAFs first combat kill when de shot down a Sabre. The next day, Flt Lt Pathania shot down the second kill over Chamb and later on the 18th, Sqn Ldr AS Sandhu despatched another over Lahore. By conflict end the squadron had also completed several close air support and bomber escort duties and ended up flying 595 sorties, totalling 455 hours. In the 1971 War they were again operating from Pathankot on CAP missions and succeeded in damaging a PAF Mirage, during a raid on their home base. PAF attacks in the 1971 War were less intense than before resulting in 338 sorties being flown by the unit, mainly on bomber escort and close air support missions. In 1979 they converted onto the MiG-21BIS and then the MiG-21UPG in February 2006. Awarded the President Standard on 13th November 1976.

▲ Sqn Ldr Raghu Raghavendran, the first Gnat squadron c/o in 1959.

▼ Panthers' MiG-21 Bison at Nasik whilst working up on the type, 2006.

Crest: A Panther standing astride the numbers 23. Designed in the late 1950's by the squadron's Flight Commander, Flt Lt Ian Loughran.

Motto: 'Amritham Abhayam / Immortal And Fearless'.

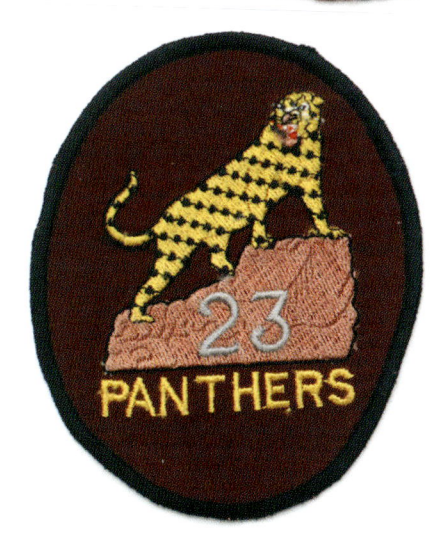

Flying Squadrons 73

23 Squadron

74 Squadrons, Patches, Heraldry & Artwork of the Indian Air Force: 1932-2016

24 SQUADRON
'HAWKS'

The Hawks were raised on the 16th February 1962 at Chabua with the Vampire and were operational during the Chinese Aggression later in the year flying combat air patrols and performing reconnaissance missions along the narrow valleys of the northeast. The squadron moved to Bareilly before transferring to Kalaikunda in time for the 1965 war with Pakistan when they were forward deployed to Barrackpore, providing air defence and close air support. Later they performed combat air patrols in the Gorakhpur region. In March 1966 the squadron converted to the Gnat at Tezpur. During the 1971 war they carried out successful ground attacks against enemy targets in East Pakistan from Tezpur and their forward airbase at Kumbhigram and later at Argatala. The 12-year association with the Gnat came to an end in April 1978, when they converted to the MiG-21M. In May 1981 they converted on to the MiG-21BIS at Ambala relinquishing them in March 1997 and going into hibernation. The squadron was resurrected at Pune as the first IAF Flanker squadron on 12th May 1997 with the Su-30K and later traded these in for the improved Su-30MKI in February 2007. Awarded the President's Standard on 6th March 2012.

▲ Wg Cdr Shetty standing in front of 24 Squadron Gnat.

▲ Pilots of 24 Squadron in the 1960's.

Crest: A Hawk swooping down towards its prey. Later variation shows bolts of lightning under the claws of the Hawk depicting the lethal firepower of the aircraft's weapons, the seven stars represent the 'Great Bear' constellation, the blue top portion the sky, the black bottom portion the sky at night and red band around the edge the colour of the battlefield.

Motto: 'Navijitya Nivartanam / No Return Without Conquest'.

▲ 24 Squadron pilots during gunnery training at Jaisalmer 1989.

76　　Squadrons, Patches, Heraldry & Artwork of the Indian Air Force: 1932-2016

24 Squadron

▲ Wg Cdr S. Asthana, c/o of 24 Squadron in 1989. His uniform apart from carrying Hawks' patches also has a shoulder tab stating 'Hawk Leader'.

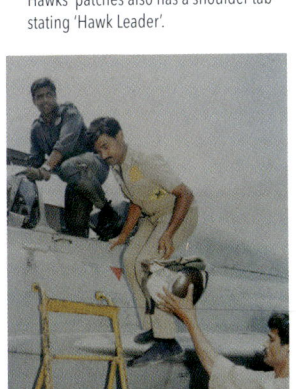

▲ Pilot gets into his MiG-21BIS during a gunnery detachment at Jaisalmer in 1992.

Flying Squadrons 77

25 SQUADRON
'THE HIMALAYAN EAGLES'

The squadron was formed on 1st March 1963 at Chandigarh with four Antonov 12 primarily for use in the high altitude Ladakh region. The squadron developed the concept of air maintenance to the northern sector developing procedures for landing at high altitude airfields such as Leh (10,682 feet), Chushul (14,500 feet) and Thoise (10,066 feet). They flew many sorties during the 1965 conflict and likewise in 1971. Notably in 1971 they participated in the Parachute drop at Tangail over East Pakistan and also trained for use of the An-12 in the bombing role. In 1989 the An-12's were supplemented by the IL-76 before being retired on 30th June 1993 in lieu of the Antonov 32. The Himalayan Eagles have continued to operate both the IL-76 and An-32 in the northern air bridge role and in disaster relief operations. During the Kargil war in 1999 they flew 1692 hours over a two and a half month period, airlifting 7500 tonnes of equipment and 26,364 troops. On 1st September 2011 the squadron relinquished its IL-76's and moved to South West Air Command. Awarded the President Standard on 18th December 2012.

Crest: The crest was approved by the President of India on 24th December 1969 and depicts the 'Himalayan Eagle' over the mighty snow capped Himalayas. The crest also carries the inscription 'Saviours of the North'.

Motto: 'Satvadeena hi Sidhvayah / Excellence Through Diligence'.

▼ 25 Squadron IL-76 at Chandigarh in 2008.   ▲ The squadron logo on an An-32.

78   Squadrons, Patches, Heraldry & Artwork of the Indian Air Force: 1932-2016

26 SQUADRON
'WARRIORS'

The Warriors were formed on the 1st January 1968 at Adampur and became the first squadron in the IAF to operate the Su-7 fighter-bomber. As is typical with most organisations around the world, the first squadron becomes the training squadron and 26 was no exception. During the 1971 War the unit was tasked with counter air missions and ground attack. During the intense activity of they lost six aircraft to a combination of ground fire and enemy air to air missiles. The unit moved onto Ambala in June 1973 where they remained until June 1977. They converted onto the MiG-21BIS in June 1977 and moved to Pathankot offering pilot training under the MOFT syllabus. Today they are the last squadron flying the MiG-21BIS and were awarded The President Standard in November 2014.

Crest: A Warrior holding a spear in aggressive mode, signifying a final blow to the vanquished enemy.

Motto: 'Yudhyasva Vigatha Jwar / Wage War With All Your Might'.

Flying Squadrons

27 SQUADRON
'FLAMING ARROWS'

The Flaming Arrows were raised on 15th February 1957 with the Vampire FB52 at Adampur. In October 1958 they converted onto the Hunter F56 at Ambala and they flew in Operation Vijay over the Portuguese enclave of Goa. During the 1965 War they operated from Halwara to where they had moved in March 1964 and flew air defence, reconnaissance and ground attack missions. Missions were conducted in the Gujranwala and Khemkaran-Kasur sectors and along the Sialkot-Lahore-Ferozpur Axis. In April 1967 all the Hunter F56's were replaced by the F56A and the squadron's role changed to that of deep penetration strike. They moved to Pathankot in July 1971, which was to be their operational base during the 1971 war. Close air support and air defence missions were the prime roles of the squadron during the conflict. They also carried out counter air strikes against the PAF airfields of Sakesar, Murid and Mianwali.

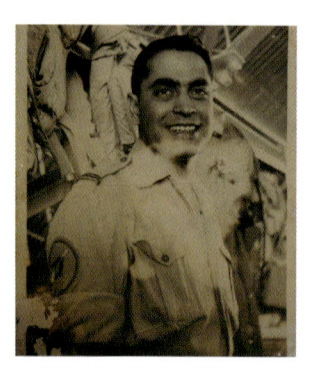

▲ 27 Squadron pilot circa 1960's.

▲ 27 Squadron logo on a preserved Hawker Hunter at Halwara.

▲ 27 Squadron deployment to Leh in 1984.

▲ The entrance to 27 Squadron HQ Complex.

80 Squadrons, Patches, Heraldry & Artwork of the Indian Air Force: 1932-2016

In December 1975 they relocated to Bhuj, followed in September 1977 to Jamnager. In June 1981 they moved east to Hashimara and in April 1984 they sent a detachment to Leh in support of Operation Meghdoot. Leh airfield is at 10,682 feet and at the time was the highest operational airfield in the world and the Hunters were the first fighter aircraft to operate from there. In January 1985 they converted onto the Jaguar at the HAL airfield in Bangalore before moving onto CAC. During the 1999 Kargil war they operated from Awantipur along with aircraft from 14 squadron. The high battlefield was not best suited to Jaguar operations; however the fleet did complete several reconnaissance missions using LOROP and Vicon pods. Awarded the President Standard on 13th November 1996.

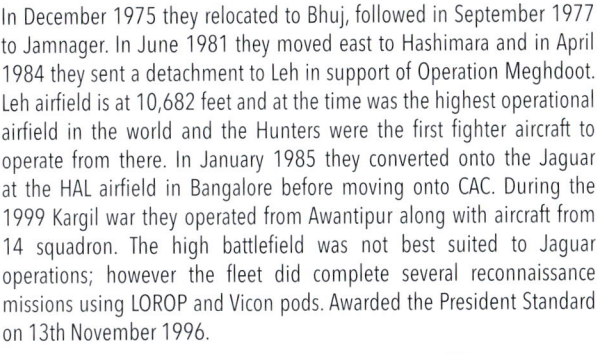

Crest: *The crest consists of a flaming arrow against a blue background. It signifies the accuracy and lethal fire power of the unit. The crest was approved by the President of India on 23rd February 1960.*

Motto: *'Durarakshya Sharlakshya / Strike Deep, Strike Hard.'*

Flying Squadrons   81

28 SQUADRON
'FIRST SUPERSONICS'

Formed at Chandigarh on 2nd March 1963, the squadron ushered in the era of supersonic fighters into the IAF. The First aircraft were delivered after reassembly at Bombay Docks in April 1963 and consisted of six MiG-21F13. In 1965, six MiG-21PF's joined the unit followed by the first of the two seaters in November 1965. During the 1965 War with Pakistan, they were stationed at Pathankot and although not fully worked up they succeeded in mounting several missions in the air defence role that included day and night CAP, fighter sweeps and interceptions. Post war they moved to Adampur and received the first MiG-21FL to join the IAF in July 1966. By the time of the 1971 War the unit were based at Tezpur in EAC and just before hostilities began they moved to Guwahati. Under the command of Wg Cdr B.K. Bishnoi they were entrusted with air defence, counter air attacks and offensive air support missions. Persistent and accurate attacks on the runways at Tezgoan and Kurmitola over the period earnt them the informal name of 'The Runway Busters'. The squadron were also given the task of offensive air support in aid

▼ 28 Squadron pilots in front of their trusty steed.

of the IA, clearing a path for them through to Dacca. They neutralised enemy armour concentrations at various ferry crossing points, destroying at the same time numerous barges that were aiding the retreat of forces. They created history on 14th December, when an eight aircraft formation attacked Dacca at tree top height, their goal being to Governor's Palace which was attacked with 57mm rocket projectiles, forcing him to resign. Thus the squadron played a very important part in the liberation of Dacca and were rightly awarded the Battle Honour 'Dacca', having flown 320 missions in the period. After the war they took on the additional role of training, ceasing to fly the MiG-21FL on 15th December 1986 when they became the second unit to convert to the MiG-29 at Pune. They remained at Pune until 2001 before moving to their current home and were awarded the President Standard on 2nd April 1991 and celebrated their Golden Anniversary in April 2013.

Crest: The squadron badge depicts the 'Sudarshan Chakra' (Ring of Fire) carried by Lord Vishnu together with a shock wave to signify the great speed at which the Chakra could move making perception of its approach difficult. This traditional Indian symbol is a weapon of destruction used to clear out evil, moving at incredible speed.

Motto: 'Samharam Cha Karoti Yah / Determined To Destroy'.

Battle Honours:

Indo-Pak Conflict 1971
Air Offensive for Liberation of Bangladesh
'Air Offensive' (Dacca)

▼ Below left: 28 Squadron MiG-29UB at Pune in 1998.
Below right: Close-up of 28 Squadron logo on MiG-29A.

Flying Squadrons   83

28 Squadron

▼ 28 Squadron wall art at Pune.

▲ 28 Squadron HQ Complex at Pune.

▲ 28 Squadron artwork in their museum.

84 — Squadrons, Patches, Heraldry & Artwork of the Indian Air Force: 1932-2016

29 SQUADRON
'SCORPIOS'

The Scorpios were raised on the Dassault Ouragon at Halwara on 10th March 1958 and were initially tasked with air defence duties. In September 1960 they moved east to bolster defences, initially going to Kalaikunda before settling at Tezpur in November 1961. In the run up to the 1965 War they also operated at Guwahati before being based at Bagdogra and from here they carried out ground support missions for the IA. After the war they moved to Adampur on 10th May 1967 and converted onto the MiG-21FL, moving onto Hindon in June 1968 to defend the nation's capitol, Delhi. In early 1971 the squadron joined with 47 squadron to form the 'Red Scorchers' aerobatic team, consisting of four aircraft which displayed at annual fire power demonstration at the Tilpat Range. During the 1971 War they deployed to Sirsa and Uttarlai from where they carried CAP missions, bomber escorts and high level fighter sweeps over the front. On 16th December Flt Lt S.V. Shah shot down a PAF Shenyang F-6 which attempted to intercept a fighter sweep over the Nayar Chor along the border. On 17th December, Sqn Ldr I.S. Bindra shot down a F-104 which was attempting to strike Uttarlai airfield.

Crest: *A Black Scorpion in offensive posture. The sting coiled up to show the enemy its lethality.*

Motto: *'Sadaiv Sachet / Ever Alert'.*

Battle Honours:

Indo-Pak Conflict 1971
Entire Operations
Air Defence

▲ 29 Squadron MiG-23UB at Jodhpur in 1998. ▼ 29 Squadron MiG-27 at Jodhpur in 1998.

▲ 29 Squadron logo as applied to aircraft pre 1999.

Flying Squadrons   85

29 Squadron

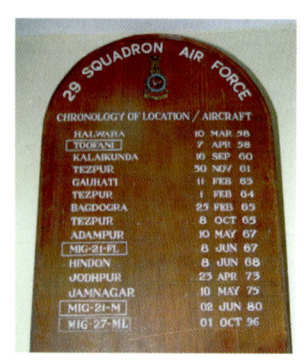

Another F-104 was jointly claimed by two pilots, Flt Lt A.K. Dutta and Flt Lt N. Kukreja while on an escort mission. Sqn Ldr K.C. Shekar, leader of the Sirsa detachment also completed a number of tactical reconnaissance missions over installations over the front. They moved to Jodhpur in the air defence role in April 1973 before moving to Jamnager in May 1975. On the 2nd June 1980 they converted onto the MiG-21M, winning the award of best combat squadron in the IAF in 1984. On 1st October 1996 they traded in their aircraft for the MiG-27 and moved to Jodhpur in 1997, later upgrading to the MiG-27UPG. Awarded the President Standard on 7th November 1997.

▲ 29 Squadron Chronology of events.

86 Squadrons, Patches, Heraldry & Artwork of the Indian Air Force: 1932-2016

30 SQUADRON
'RHINOS'

The Rhinos were formed on the 1st November 1969 at Tezpur on the MiG-21FL. During the 1971 war with Pakistan, they maintained deployments at Kalaikunda and Panagarh in the east and during the first day on the 4th September they were dog fighting with Pakistani F86's over Dacca. A week later the squadron was split in two and despatched to Pathankot and Chandigarh in the western sector. They maintained aircraft at operational readiness alert and engaged the enemy on numerous occasions, but without success. After the war they returned to the east and were stationed at Kalaikunda from where they moved to Tezpur in 1973. The squadron was numberplated on the 31st October 2002, exactly 33 years to the date on formation. The unit reformed on the Su-30MKI in April 2004.

▲ 30 Squadron MiG-21FL at Tezpur in 2000.

▲ Rhino logo on a MiG-21FL.

Flying Squadrons

Crest: *The unit emblem depicts a one horned grey Rhino over two Naga spears. The Rhino is commonly found in the state of Assam and signifies strength and courage, whilst the Naga spears symbolise fearlessness and fierceness when aroused.*

Motto: *'Aseema Paurusha / Boundless Valour'.*

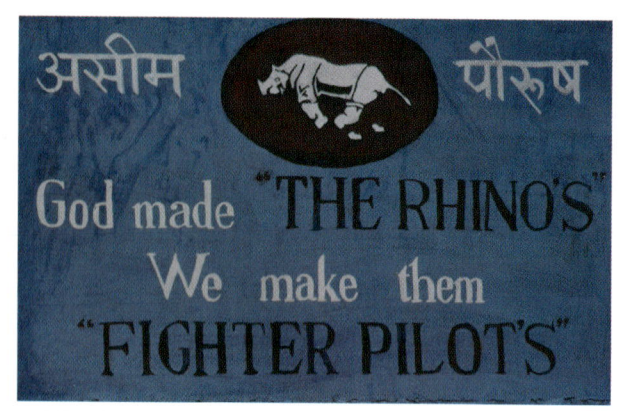

▲ 30 Squadron signage at Tezpur circa 2000, when they had the added task of stage 3 pilot training.

88 Squadrons, Patches, Heraldry & Artwork of the Indian Air Force: 1932-2016

30 Squadron

Flying Squadrons

31 SQUADRON
'LIONS'

The squadron was raised at Pathankot on 1st September 1963 on the Mystere IVA. During the 1965 war they flew 41 sorties in ground attack missions, primarily in the Chamb-Janarian Sector. Later they operated in other areas including Chawind, Sialkot and Pasrur and also completed reconnaissance missions. In July 1971 the Lions moved onto Hindon, from where they were based during 1971 operations. At the onset they despatched a detachment of six aircraft to Sirsa from where they flew 165 sorties over a two week period. As before their mission was ground attack and reconnaissance. In 1973 they converted onto the Marut and later in May 1975 moved to Jodhpur. They continued with the Marut until April 1983 and converted onto the MiG-23BN at Halwara. During Kargil operations in 1999 they deployed to Nal in the South West Sector whereupon they flew several reconnaissance and electronic warfare missions. Two pilots from the squadron were detached to 221 squadron and flew combat missions over the high altitude battle zone. The squadron were numberplated on 1st October 2003 with the advent of the MiG-23BN force drawdown. They were resurrected on 1st January 2009 on the Su-30MKI and awarded the President Standard on 8th January 2011.

Crest: The image of a mountain Lion in a crouching stance, ready to pounce on its prey. The depiction symbolising the squadron's ever alert poise and lethality, and its ability to strike hard and deep into enemy territory.

Motto: 'Shatrum Chhidrey Praharet / A kill with every blow.'

Battle Honours:

Indo-Pak Conflict 1965
A) Armour Thrust by Pakistan Chhamb-Jourian
B) Lahore Kasur Sector Lahore Kasur

Indo-Pak Conflict 1971 (West Pakistan)
Air Offensive West Pakistan
Air Offensive

▶ 31 Squadron logo as painted on a preserved MiG-23BN at Halwara.

Squadrons, Patches, Heraldry & Artwork of the Indian Air Force: 1932-2016

31 Squadron

▲ 31 Squadron pilots and Marut circa 1970's.

Flying Squadrons 91

31 Squadron

▲ 31 Squadron MiG-23UB.

32 SQUADRON
'THUNDERBIRDS'

The unit was formed at Hindon in November 1963 with the Vampire FB52 which turned out to be an interim measure as they re-equipped with the Mystere IV in 1964. During the 1965 War they were tasked with close air support and battlefield air interdiction from Adampur in the area of the Ichogil Canal which ran parallel to the Atari-Lahore road link which was the road between Gujarat and Wazirabad and rear assembly areas near Chawinda. In 1969 they converted onto the Su-7 and moved to Ambala and deployed out to Amritsar on the eve of the 1971 conflict. They commenced the war by mounting counter air strikes against the PAF airfields of Shortkot Road and Sargodha, claiming several aircraft destroyed on the ground. During these missions they lost three aircraft with the pilots being captured. On 6th December, Flt Lt M. Malhotra claimed a capping Shenyang F-6 whilst on a low-hi-low tactical reconnaissance mission over Chandler Airfield. On the 9th December the squadron switched to close air support in the Chhamb and Shakargarh sector, flying a total of 127 missions during the entire conflict over 14 days. The unit moved to Hindon in the late 70s before converting onto the MiG-21BIS in January 1984 in SWAC where they remain to this day having converted onto the MiG-21UPG in 2005. Awarded the President Standard on 20th November 2013.

Crest: A Thunderbird (non native Indian bird) named by the squadron c/o whilst it was at Ambala in 1978. W/Co AJS Sandhu has served at Nellis AFB in 1963 and witnessed the 'Thunderbirds' aerobatic team.

Motto: 'Mahavegashya Dhundvrataha / Fast in speed, fast in determination.'

▼ 32 Squadron flight crew atop one of their Su-7's.

Flying Squadrons 93

32 Squadron

▲ 32 Squadron Su-7 along with the entire squadron personnel.

▲ 32 Squadron logo painted on a building.

94   Squadrons, Patches, Heraldry & Artwork of the Indian Air Force: 1932-2016

32 Squadron

Flying Squadrons 95

33 SQUADRON
'HIMALAYAN GEESE'

The Geese were raised on 9th January 1963 at Guwahati with DHC Caribou aircraft. This unit was specifically inducted with this STOL aircraft to operate in the challenging conditions of the NEFA. Being a versatile aircraft, the Caribou was able to operate into the short field Air Landing Grounds of Arunachal Pradesh, Nagaland and Mizo Hills. The squadron used them for transportation, casualty evacuation, Para dropping, reconnaissance, survey, SAR and communications. During the 1971 War it was involved in supply drops over East Pakistan and they also took part in the Tangail Para drop. Unusually 33 squadron's aircraft were employed in nocturnal nuisance air raids on Pakistani installations in Dacca, dropping 500 lb and 1000 lbs bombs. The Caribou was phased out in 1987, being replaced by the An-32. In 1991 the squadron moved south to Sulur, where it was numberplated on 31st July 1991. It was later re-established on the 27th March 2000 with the An-32, later taking part in relief operations after the Bhuj Earthquake in 2001 and the Asian Tsunami in 2004. They were awarded the President Standard on 18th December 2012.

Crest: A single Goose flying over the Himalayas.

Motto: 'Shramo Dadati Siddim / Through hardwork comes Glory'.

◀ 33 Squadron logo as painted on an An-32.

Squadrons, Patches, Heraldry & Artwork of the Indian Air Force: 1932-2016

35 SQUADRON
RAPIERS

The Rapiers were raised on 10th August 1958 at Pune on the Canberra B(I)58. The unit saw operational service in Operation Vijay, the Indian reclamation of former Portuguese Territory and dropped 60,000 lbs of bombs over Goa. During the 1965 War they flew 69 sorties dropping 350,000 lbs of bombs over East and West Pakistan. The highlights of which were counter air missions against Sargodha between the 7th and 10th September. During the 1971 War they again completed a variety of bombing missions on both fronts accumulating 92 operational sorties along the way, dropping 630,000 lbs of bombs and losing one aircraft. Targets included Karachi Harbour, Manora Fort, several rail junctions of strategic importance and the enemy airfields at Sargodha, Masroor, Nawa Bshah and Drigh Road. On the night of the 5th December the unit attacked the oil storage tanks at Kiamari which remained burning for one week after the attack. In January 1978 the unit was specially selected to change over to the electronic warfare role with two flights; A Flight was equipped with modified Canberras and B Flight with the MiG-21M. Moving to Bareilly in their new role the squadron had the opportunity to face new challenges resulting in its specialisation in the stand off jamming and escort jamming roles. The special Canberras left the squadron in January 1998 to go to 106 squadron at Agra. The squadron took part in Operation Safed Sager over Kargil and over the deserts of South West Air Command in its specialist capacity as the electronic warfare escort squadron. They lost their electronic warfare role in 2001 and in 2003 the remnants from 102 squadron flying the MiG-25 were amalgamated into the squadron, becoming their A flight. Therefore the unit was operational again with two flights and two types. The MiG-25 finally retired in May 2005 and 35 squadron moved from Bareilly to Bakshi Ke Talab in 2006. There they took over the operational role of Air Defence Flight and today continue in the air defence and bombing role. Awarded the President Standard on 24th October 2000.

Crest: An erect Rapier.

Motto: 'Drutapraharanayudh / Armed To Strike Fast'.

▼ 35 Squadron MiG-21M in 2010.

Flying Squadrons   97

35 Squadron

▲ 35 Squadron 'B' Flight MiG-21 pilots.

37 SQUADRON
"BLACK PANTHERS"

The Black Panthers as they are well known in the IAF were formed on 23rd December 1957 at Palam flying the Vampire NF10 night fighter. In February 1960 the unit moved to Pune and converted onto the Hunter on 15th November 1962, later moving east to Chabua on 16th February 1964. Prior to the 1965 War the assets of the unit were split with four aircraft being sent to provide air defence at Guwahati and the remainder being sent west to Hindon. In the East they were able to launch offensive strikes against the airfield at Kurmitola and from Hindon they mounted combat air patrols over the capital, Delhi. Post war saw them re-uniting at Chabua and then moving onto Tezpur in March 1966 until another move to Hashimara on 20th March 1968. Whilst stationed there the unit performed well in the 1971 War flying a total of 187 missions comprising of fighter reconnaissance, counter air and close air support. During this conflict they lost two Hunters to ground fire, but were credited a Sabre kill to Flying Office H Masand over Dacca on 4th December. On 21st December 1973 they moved to Kalaikunda and then onto Adampur for conversion onto the MiG-21M in February 1977. Staying at Adampur for six years, they moved onto Chandigarh in April 1983 staying until February 1985. Their next home was Nal when they were given the additional role of conducting the MOFT syllabus before settling into the rebuilt Bhuj airbase on 7th April 2003. They were awarded the President Standard on 15th February 2007.

▼ 37 Squadron MiG-21M awaiting ground power from the APA-5D.

Crest: A pouncing Black Panther.

Motto: 'Sadaiv Nirbhik / Forever Fearless'

Battle Honours:
Indo-Pak Conflict 1971 (East Pakistan)
Air Offensive for Liberation of Bangladesh - Air Offensive

◀▲ 37 Squadron pilots at rest, circa 1960's.

100 Squadrons, Patches, Heraldry & Artwork of the Indian Air Force: 1932-2016

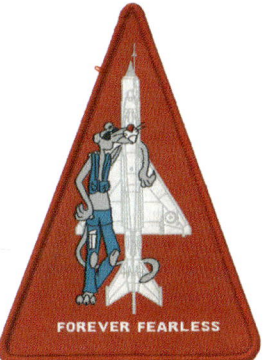

37 Squadron

Flying Squadrons

37 Squadron

▲ 37 Squadron pilots circa 2000's whilst conducting stage 3 'MOFT' syllabus.

▲ 37 Squadron commanding officers.

102 Squadrons, Patches, Heraldry & Artwork of the Indian Air Force: 1932-2016

41 SQUADRON
'OTTERS'

The Otters were raised on 1st March 1958 at Jodhpur on the DHC-3 Otter. Their primary role has been to supply logistics air support, casualty evacuation, photo reconnaissance and supply dropping to the military and civil authorities. During Operation Vijay they supplied a detachment of aircraft to support ground forces in the Portuguese enclave of Goa. In the 1962 conflict with China they flew 705 operational sorties in Arunanchal Pradesh, which gave vital support to the Indian Army. During the 1965 war they flew a total of 614 missions and later, during the 1971 war they flew 162 missions. During the Naga insurgency in the North Eastern Frontier Authority region, several of the units' Otters were converted to fire rockets from underwing pods and to fire machine guns through cabin windows. The Otters were phased out in 1984 and replaced by the Dornier 228, becoming the first unit to operate the type. These were joined by several HS-748 in 1996. They were awarded the President Standard on 7th November 1997.

Crest: An Otter signifying the single minded devotion to the task in hand irrespective of the prevailing conditions ensuring that help reaches those in need on time.

Motto: 'Samay par Sahayta / Help in Time.'

▲ 41 Squadron Dornier 228 visiting Agra in 2003.

Flying Squadrons   103

42 SQUADRON

Crest: An Eagle carrying bushels.

Motto: 'Seva Rakshyanaya / Serve & Protect.'

The squadron was formed on 7th March 1961 with the Ilyushin 14 at Palam in Delhi. They later moved onto Srinagar and then Chandigarh, before going to Sarsawa and ending up back at Palam where they were numberplated in 1974, following the withdrawal of the IL-14 from service. The early days saw the squadron primarily involved in servicing the air bridge between Chandigarh and Leh, but the lack of payload capability on the IL-14 meant that it was quickly relegated to performing such tasks as ferrying VIP's, transporting urgent spares and running courier services. During the 1971 War, 42 squadron performed several tasks including personnel movement and casualty evacuation, at which it excelled. In the latter mode it was able to accommodate 18 full stretcher loads together with six ambulance cases.

▲ 42 Squadron IL-14's possibly taken at a RAF Station in the Gulf circa 1960's.

43 SQUADRON
IBEXES

The Ibexes were raised at Barrackpore on 20th January 1958 on the C-47 merging with 48 squadron in 1960. Temporarily numberplated they resurrected almost immediately on the Dakota IV, that had modifications which enabled the unit to operate at higher altitude. Consequently in 1960 they moved to Jammu & Kashmir, operating from the bases of Srinagar and Jammu, later moving onto Sarsawa in September 1965. During the 1965 War they operated at Srinagar and undertook over 600 missions including casualty evacuation, transport and communications. In 1967 they moved to Jorhat in order to undertake air maintenance of the North East Frontier Agency. During the 1971 War they undertook clandestine missions over East Pakistan and took part with six aircraft in the Tangail Para Drop on 6th December. The last Dakota was retired on 31st March 1985, by which time the squadron was working up on the An-32, the first of which had arrived on 18th September 1984. They flew operations in support of the IPKF over Sri Lanka in 1987 and in November 1988 took part in operations over Male. They were awarded the President Standard on 10th March 1992.

Crest: The squadron crest was approved on 9th April 1962 and consists of an Ibex head on a Chinar leaf, with the Ashoka seal placed on top. The Ibex is a mountain goat found in the Jammu & Kashmir region, which is undeterred by the jagged rocks, steep cliffs, inhospitable terrain and forbidding snow of the challenging Himalayas. These were qualities that symbolised the activities and inhospitable conditions that the squadron operated in.

Motto: 'Nabhsa Jeevan Dhara / A Lifeline Through The Sky'.

44 SQUADRON
'MIGHTY JETS'

The squadron was raised on 6th April 1961 at Chandigarh, when the first of 8 Antonov 12s were inducted into the IAF. During the 4 week war with China in 1962 they operated around the clock in the Ladakh area of Kashmir airlifting supplies into high altitude airfields and drop zones. During the 1965 Indo-Pak War they were active with strategic and tactical airlift missions. In 1971 they looked into the possibility of the Antonov 12 being converted into bombers by means of an internal conveyor belt. By the time of the commencement of hostilities in December, this had become reality. With conflict approaching both Antonov 12 squadrons at Chandigarh moved out, with 25 Squadron going to Nagpur and then onto Gorakhpur and 44 Squadron going to Bareilly. Over a six day period starting on the 3rd December they performed bombing missions over targets in West Pakistan. Thereafter 6 aircraft flew to Calcutta where they prepared for a major airborne assault in East Pakistan, which took place on the 11th when they dropped heavy equipment over Tangail. The next day they performed a daylight raid against an ordnance factory in this sector before returning west, taking part in another four bombing missions over targets in West Pakistan between 12th and 17th December. In between the bombing, ordinary strategic and tactical transport missions

▼ 44 Squadron IL-76 gets underway at Yelehanka Air Base, near Bangalore.

had to be performed. Antonov 12 aircraft of 44 Squadron also provided long range maritime reconnaissance and an aircraft was converted to be an Airborne Command Post. For its performance during the war it became the first transport squadron to receive a battle honour. In March 1985 they converted to the IL-76. This was particularly useful in airlifting troops of the Indian Peace-Keeping Force that were sent to Sri Lanka between 1987 and 1989. The squadron airlifted troops of the 6th Battalion, Parachute Regiment, 2,000 kms non-stop to secure the International Airport and government buildings in the Maldives Islands following a revolt on 3rd November 1988. The squadron moved to Agra in 1989, this being the home of 12 squadron and PTS. Many of the armies parachute formations are headquartered here as well. Relief missions now play an important part in squadron life. From the Siachen Glacier to floods in Assam, the Gujarat Earthquake in 2001, overseas relief missions to Armenia, Bangladesh and Afghanistan are now all unfortunately regular occurrences. Awarded President's Standard on 9th March 2011.

Crest: *A Goose flying against the background of the Himalayas. Also known as the 'Mighty Jets' since the induction of the IL-76.*

Motto: *'Ishtam Yatnen Sadhyet / Fly Safe, Fly Smart'.*

Battle Honours:
Indo-Pak Conflict 1971 (West Pakistan)
Air Offensive West Pakistan
Air Offensive

▲ 44 Squadron An-12 possibly depicting missions flown in the 1971 War.

Flying Squadrons 107

45 SQUADRON
'FLYING DAGGERS'

The Flying Daggers were raised at Palam in January 1960 with Vampire FB52's inherited from 23 sqn. During Operation Vijay over Goa in 1961 two aircraft from the squadron attacked a Portuguese Patrol boat. Prior to the 1965 war they were stationed at Pune offering initial jet training, however the dark clouds of war saw them posted to Pathankot where they undertook ground attack missions operating jointly with 220 squadron. However they suffered badly on their first operational sortie losing four aircraft and three pilots killed in action over Chhamb on 1st September 1965. In August 1966 they became the second squadron to convert to the MiG-21FL at Chandigarh and took on the mantle of training squadron. By June 1985 they were operating the MiG-21M. By April 1990 they were operating the MiG-21BIS and were based at Naliya between 1986 and 2002. Whilst at Naliya, an aircraft from the Flying Daggers shot down an over flying PAF Atlantic on 10th August 1999, the pilot Sqn Ldr Bundella later dying in a MiG-21 accident. The squadron were numberplated and were resurrected as the first Tejas squadron on 1st July 2016.

Crest: *A Dagger over a set of wings, which was approved by the President on 16th September 1961.*

Motto: *"Ajeeta Nabaha / Shining In The Sky".*

◀ 45 Squadron pilot in front of a squadron MiG-21BIS.

108 — Squadrons, Patches, Heraldry & Artwork of the Indian Air Force: 1932-2016

47 SQUADRON
'BLACK ARCHERS'

The unit was formed on 18th December 1959 at Halwara airbase flying the Ouragon. In 1962 they moved to Kalaikunda and later in August 1963 onto Bagdogra. In September 1965 they proceeded to Hashimara which was to be their home base during the 1965 War. During September they sent detachments to Tezpur and Guwahati, where they performed air defence. After the conflict they moved to Chandigarh in March 1968 and converted onto the MiG-21FL. Hindon was their next base where they stayed from February 1969 until November 1973. In early 1971 AIRHQ decided to raise a MiG-21 aerobatic team of personnel from 29 and 47 squadron. Three pilots were to be selected from each squadron under the command of Wg Cdr H.S. Gill, c/o of 47 squadron and former flight commander of 29 squadron. The initial cadre under Gill included Sqn Ldr V Kapila, Sqn Ldr D.S. Sant, Sqn Ldr U.V. Lagad, Sqn Ldr A.K.M. Raje, Sqn Ldr I.J.S. Bopari and Flt Lt A.K. Singh. These pilots progressively worked up to two ship, three and finally four ship formations. Wg Cdr H.S. Gill was also to perform single aircraft low level aerobatics. A name was decided upon which was a mix of the names of 29 and 47 squadrons, and henceforth they were to be known as 'The Red Scorchers'. During work up it was decided that the basic natural metal finish of the aircraft was deemed to be unsuitable. The senior engineering officer from 28 wing at Hindon was asked to explore the possibilities of painting the aircraft without damage to the surface. Sqn Ldr V. Kapila suggested that they use distemper instead

▲ 47 Squadron, one off low viz crest on a MiG-29.

▲ 47 Squadron MiG-29A taken in 2008.

Flying Squadrons 109

Crest: *Their crest depicts a kneeling archer with drawn bow and has been chosen for its suggestion of poised readiness. Its significance as a crest is that it is symbolic of the aim for fine training and absolute preparedness for the appointed task.*

Motto: *'Karmani Vyarutam Dhanuhu / Bow must always be stretched for the task.'*

of normal paint as there was no danger of corrosion. After much debate and experimentation, it was decided that red would be the most suitable colour. There after aircraft with the best serviceability rate were selected for re-painting in dry distemper which could be washed off at any time. The low level display aircraft received another colour scheme using two colours plus two eyes painted on either side of the forward fuselage. One eye would be open and one closed and it was hoped that this would create a winking eye effect as the singleton completed low level aerobatics. Air Vice Marshall Vinay Kapila speaking later in retirement described the five minute display of the team. 'The final pattern comprised of a run in along the audience, pulling up for a loop and feeding straight into a right hand wing over followed by a barrel roll to the left and coming out of the barrel roll into a right wing over followed by another loop. From this loop we went into another loop that culminated in the downward 'bomb burst'. We had found that in order to make the bomb burst more spectacular, we needed to engage afterburners as we came vertically down and did a snap 90 degree turn outwards and pulled out in four different directions disappearing from vision of the audience'. The low level solo aerobatic display by Wg Cdr H.S. Gill was just as spectacular. It included an inverted flypast, the 'twinkle roll' showing the winking eyes of either side of the fuselage to good effect, loops, barrel rolls and eight point rolls. During the 1971 war 47 squadron despatched aircraft to Jamnager, Halwara, Palam and Hindon for the duration of the war, their main task being that of air

110 Squadrons, Patches, Heraldry & Artwork of the Indian Air Force: 1932-2016

defence and counter air missions. One of the Jamnager detachments was shot down on a counter air mission over Badin Airfield and unfortunately the squadron commander Wg Cdr H.S. Gill, the solo display pilot and leader of the Scorchers lost his life. Another aircraft was lost in a landing accident on the 12th, when F/O P.K. Sahu undershot the runway at Palam, whilst part of the Delhi detachment. On the 12th December another of the Jamnager detachment, Sqn Ldr B.B. Soni shot down a F-104 off the coast. In November 1973 they moved to Halwara and then east to Chabua in January 1978. Here they stayed until May 1985 moving to Hashimara before numberplating in October 1986, when its pilots were sent to the Soviet Union for conversion to the MiG-29. In May 1987 they were resurrected as the first MiG-29 squadron at Pune. Awarded the President Standard on 10th November 2009.

48 SQUADRON
'CAMELS'

The Camels were raised on the 19th November 1959 at Srinagar on the C-47. The squadron moved to Barrackpore on 24th May 1960 and converted onto the C-119 on 1st February 1962. In June 1963 they moved to Kalaikunda and then onto Allahabad in June 1968. Whilst at Allahabad they maintained a detachment at Kumbhigram in support of ground forces operating against insurgents in the Mizo Hills. In 1985 they re-equipped with the Antonov 32 and moved to their current location at Chandigarh in May 1986. Since then they have been performing air maintenance role in the Jammu & Kashmir area and notably on 31st May 2008 became the first unit to operate into the recently reactivated air landing ground at Daulat Beg Oldie (16,614') for 46 years. The squadron has participated in most of the IAF operations since inception in 1959. Notably in the war with China in 1962 they operated in the Eastern sector, airlifting troops and military hardware. During the Indo-Pak War on 1965 they were actively engaged in the airlifting of troops and armament in both the Eastern and Western Sectors. During 1971 operations they were allotted the task of supporting the guerrilla movement known as the Mukti-Bahini in East Pakistan form the forward airbase at Argatala. They also provided aircraft for the parachute drop over Tangail. Between April

▼ 48 Squadron An-32 at Chandigarh in 2008.

and May 1987 they participated in Operation Pawan in support of Indian peace keeping troops operating in Sri Lanka and in 1999 they participated in Operation Safed Sagar in support of IAF and Indian Army formations operating in the Kargil War. They were awarded the President Standard on 27th February 2007. Awarded President Standard on 15th February 2007.

▲ 48 Squadron C-119 crews during a staff visit.

Crest: *A Camel, which symbolizes grit and resilience in carrying out their assigned task in the harshest imaginable conditions and inhospitable terrain, often at or beyond the aircraft's manoeuvring envelope. The crest was sanctioned by the President of India on 29th September 1969.*

Motto: *'Sahasam Falati Sarvatraha / The Courageous Always Succeed'. Also use 'Saviours of the North'*

▲ 48 Squadron An-32 landing at Daulat Beg Oldie in 2008.

Flying Squadrons 113

49 SQUADRON
'PARASPEARS'

The Paraspears were formed on 2nd February 1960 at Barrackpore with the C-47 and were tasked with air maintenance and transport support in the Eastern Sector. In May 1962 they moved to Jorhat and during the 1962 conflict with China the squadron performed admirably in difficult conditions, delivering vital supplies to troops in the Tawang Valley. Similarly during the 1965 war, they flew missions in the Eastern Sector and in 1971 they supplied six aircraft for participation in the Tangail parachute drop over East Pakistan. In 1984 the Antonov 32 joined the unit and both continued together until the faithful Dakota was retired on 31st March 1985. The Paraspears actively took part in Operation Pawan in Sri Lanka between 1987 and 1989 and for the last 20 years they have supported the civilian government with aid related flights, most notably during the Orissa Flood of 1999 and the Indian Ocean Tsunami in 2004. They were awarded the President's Standard on 9th March 2010.

Crest: The squadron crest consists of a pair of wings, a parachute, two stalks of grain and a Naga spear. These symbolise their flying, the role of airdropping, the aid to remote areas and the combat weapon of the Eastern Sector.

Motto: 'Dhairya Vijayate / Bold Will Be Victorious.'

▲ 49 Squadron crew check their charts whilst on the ground at Tezpur.

114 Squadrons, Patches, Heraldry & Artwork of the Indian Air Force: 1932-2016

50 SQUADRON

The squadron was raised on 27th May 2009 on the Beriev A-50. The A-50 is equipped with the Phalcon Airborne Warning, Control and Command System manufactured in Israel.

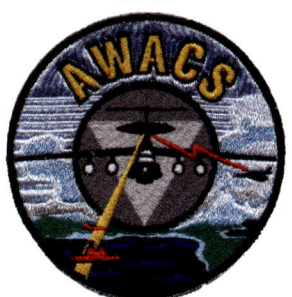

Crest: -

Motto: -

▼ 50 Squadron Beriev A-50 at Hindon in 2015 for Air Force Day.

Flying Squadrons 115

51 SQUADRON
"SWORDARMS"

The number 51 had previously been used by the IAF as an auxiliary squadron in the 1950s. Its first use as a frontline squadron started on 17th February 1985 when they were established at Chandigarh with MiG-21M's handed over from 7 squadron. They converted to the MiG-21BIS and later saw service in the Kargil War, operating from their home base in WAC and detached at Awantipur. They converted onto the MiG-21UPG.

Crest: A pair of forearms clasping a sword in aggressive fashion.

Motto: "Yudhya Mahaspara Bhayankara / Invincible In The Skies'.

Battle Honours:
Indo-Pak Conflict 1999
Operation Safed Sagar

116 Squadrons, Patches, Heraldry & Artwork of the Indian Air Force: 1932-2016

52 SQUADRON
'SHARKS'

52 squadron are the youngest fighter squadron in the Indian Air Force and were raised at Hashimara on the 1st January 1986; inheriting the MiG-21FL's of 1 Squadron that had converted onto the Mirage 2000. The squadron moved to Bagdogra during January 1990 and then moved to Chabua on the 1st November 1996. The primary role of the squadron was air defence and the secondary was ground attack. However during peacetime the squadron was given the additional responsibility of conducting the MOFT syllabus for junior pilots. Like the other operational squadrons, 52 were also forward deployed to the west during times of tension in 1987 and 1999. The unit stood down on the MiG-21FL in June 2005 and were later resurrected as the squadron number given to the Surayakiran display team flying the HAL Kiran MK2. They were numberplated in 2011 (see also Suryakiran page 217).

Crest: The squadron badge is a shark signifying the aggressive nature of fighter pilots and the ability to work as part of a team, and its ability to foray close to the shores to strike blood and terror.

Motto: 'Sadaiva Sarvottam / Always The Best'.

▲ 52 Squadron signage at Chabua in 2002.

▲ 52 Squadron logo on a MiG-21FL.

Flying Squadrons 117

AUXILIARY AIR FORCE SQUADRONS

The Indian Parliament passed the Reserve and Auxiliary Air Forces Act in August 1952, which provided for the establishment of three different categories of reserves. The third category was to be the Auxiliary Air Force; a voluntary organisation which would consist of members that could serve part time whilst following their civilian occupations. These members would receive their training at weekends and holidays and would be located in major cities where the personnel could be recruited. No 51 (Delhi) Auxiliary AF Squadron was raised on 1st November 1955 at Safdarjang Airport, followed by No 52 (Bombay) Auxiliary Air Force Squadron which was raised at Juhu on 26th May 1956. No 53 (Madras) was raised at Meenambakkam in 1956, followed by No 54 (Uttar Pradesh) at Manauri, Allahabad, No 55 (Bengal) at Barrackpore, then No 56 (Bhubaneshwar) and finally No 57 (Chandigarh) at Chandigarh. Each squadron was commanded by a serving officer and included flying instructors and technicians supplied by the IAF. Initial equipment consisted of Tiger Moths, Harvards and Prentices, but later these were replaced in some squadrons by Vampire FB52 and T55 aircraft. Following the war with China in 1962, the IAF began an expansion exercise that required the auxiliary squadrons to be absorbed into the main order of battle. Consequently all units were amalgamated into 220 and 221 squadrons flying the Vampire.

▲ 51 (Delhi) Squadron pilots in front of one of their Harvards.

▼ 51 (Delhi) Squadron just after their formation in 1955. The Sikh officer was the first Auxiliary Officer to be commissioned and a former WWII veteran.

118 Squadrons, Patches, Heraldry & Artwork of the Indian Air Force: 1932-2016

Auxiliary Air Force Squadrons

▲ A Percival Prentice as used by many auxiliary squadrons, pictured here over the UK prior to delivery.

▲ 55 (Bengal) Squadron pilots in front of their Vampire T55 in 1960.

▲ A Vampire FB52 of 51 Squadron in the late 1950's.

Flying Squadrons 119

59 SQUADRON
'HORNBILLS'

Raised in 1958 at Dinjan on DHC-3 Otter. Later they moved to Guwahati in October 1962 and inducted the entire 11th Infantry Brigade from Tezu to Walong in support of the China war effort. During the conflict the Otters flew 982 hours, airlifting 414 tonnes of material and 2083 troops. The Otter was phased out on 31st March 1991 and they converted onto the Dornier 228. Later they converted onto the HS-748. Awarded President Standard on 12th November 2008.

Crest: A Hornbill bird.

Motto: *'Nishta Dhairya Parisramah / Loyalty, Boldness and Hardwork'*

▶ 59 Squadron HS-748 at Tezpur in 2002.

▲ 59 Squadron DHC-3 Otter circa 1980's.

▲ 59 Squadron postage frank.

120   Squadrons, Patches, Heraldry & Artwork of the Indian Air Force: 1932-2016

77 SQUADRON
'VEILED VIPERS'

The squadron was raised on 5th February 2011 in WAC on the C-130J. On 20th August 2013 an aircraft from the unit landed at Daulat Beg Oldie at 16,614 feet, the world's highest airstrip. The role of the squadron involves the rapid forward deployment of personnel and equipment in emergency situations. This would include airdrops and landings on unprepared surfaces. The next C-130J squadron to stand up will be number 87 at Panagarh Air Force Station which has recently been renamed as 'Arjan Singh Air Force Station'.

Crest: A Viper's head.

Motto: 'Strike To Kill'.

▲ 77 Squadron C-130J at Yelahanka during Aero India in 2013.

Flying Squadrons 121

78 SQUADRON
'THE VALOROUS MARS'

The squadron was raised on 16th December 2003 in CAC on the Ilyushin IL-78MKI. The name comes from the acronym for the Mid Air Refuelling Squadron (MARS). The squadron has participated in several overseas deployments in support of IAF fighters and at home has taken part in various civil relief operations, notably in Carnicobar and Port Blair during the Asian Tsunami of 2005.

Crest: An Eagle, the symbol of the IAF flying over the red planet.

Motto: 'Valorous Mars'.
Also 'Steadfastness, Excellence, Valour'.

122 Squadrons, Patches, Heraldry & Artwork of the Indian Air Force: 1932-2016

81 SQUADRON
'SKYLORDS'

The Skylords were raised in WAC with the C-17 on 1st September 2013. Its primary role is that of transporting troops, equipment and supplies, either point to point or by airdrop.

Crest: The God Atlas holding up the Earth on his shoulders, with India at the centre.

Motto: 'Saksham, Balam, Sarvatram / Capable, Powerful, Omnipresent.'

▼ 81 Squadron C-17 at Yelahanka in 2015.

Flying Squadrons   123

101 SQUADRON
'FALCONS'

The Falcons can trace their lineage back to the second oldest unit in the IAF, namely number 1 Coastal Defence Flight (IAFVR) which was raised on 15th December 1940. This was later re-designated as 101 Coastal Defence Flight and later became 101 General Reconnaissance Flight on 1st December 1942. The unit was raised again at Palam on 1st May 1949, flying two Spitfire Mk.XVIIIe's and a Harvard. The basic role of the unit was to perform photo recon missions from various locations and it went onto receive several Spitfire Mk.XIX's. After receiving six of these the flight was upgraded to squadron status in April 1950. The Spitfire soldiered on for another seven years with the last flight being on 10th September 1957. They moved to Adampur and converted onto the Vampire T11 which had been converted to the PR role, later receiving the Vampire FB52 and in doing so added the ground attack role. In the late 50s they moved east to Tezpur from where they conducted missions against Naga Guerrillas in the NEFA region. During the 1965 War they remained on standby at Tezpur and also maintained a detachment at Kalaikunda. One of the squadron pilots was sent to Jamnager in the west to perform photo reconnaissance missions and succeeded in bring back tell tale evidence of Pakistani Armour movements. In June 1968 they converted onto

▼ 101 Squadron pilot about to embark on a training mission in a MiG-21UM.

124 Squadrons, Patches, Heraldry & Artwork of the Indian Air Force: 1932-2016

the Su-7 at Adampur and became the second supersonic bomber squadron in the IAF. During the 1971 War they flew 201 sorties consisting mainly of ground attack missions in support of the IA, but also counter air strikes against airfields in West Pakistan, such as Chander, photo reconnaissance and interdiction against railway yards. They lost four aircraft during the war, one shot down by a Mirage, two to ground fire and one operational accident. They converted onto the MiG-21M in July 1974 and between August 1976 and July 1978 offered type training before reverting back to their operational role. In May 1981 they moved to Sirsa and began offering the MOFT syllabus again in 1992. In 2008 they moved to Naliya and later to Jodhpur, where they were numberplated in 2012. Awarded the President Standard on 19th November 1975.

Crest: The squadron crest consists of a trained Falcon whose keen eyesight and quick kill ability symbolizes the role for which the squadron was originally formed.

Motto: 'Anwishyavedhi / Search and Destroy'. Also known as 'The Falcons of Chhamb' after their 1971 war exploits.

Battle Honours:

Indo-Pak Conflict (West Pakistan)
Pak Offensive (J&K Sector)
Chhamb-Akhnoor

Flying Squadrons   125

102 SQUADRON
'TRISONICS'

102 Survey Flight was formed at Barrackpore in December 1951 with one B-24. In February 1952, 2 Dakotas were added and the unit moved to Palam in August of that year, whereupon two Doves were added which lasted until November 1954. The flight moved back to Barrackpore in January 1956 and they became a full squadron a year later. In September 1959 they were merged into 106 (SR) squadron. They were reformed at Bareilly on 17th August 1981 with the MiG-25RB and MiG-25RU. The squadron ceased to exist in 2003 when the assets were transferred to 35 squadron. The squadron was reformed in March 2011 and now fly the Su-30MKI.

Crest: *An Eagle over a MiG-25, which became a Su-30MKI.*

Motto: *'Samdhanam Ripudamanayah / Uniting To Defeat The Enemy.'*

▲ Squadron markings on the MiG-25BR.

▲ Preserved MiG-25RB at Bareilly in 2011.

▼ 102 Squadron pilots in front of the ultra secret HQ Complex at Bareilly.

126 Squadrons, Patches, Heraldry & Artwork of the Indian Air Force: 1932-2016

104 SQUADRON
'PIONEER ROTORIONS'

Formed on 10th March 1954 on the Sikorsky S-55 at Palam, their lineage can be traced back to number 4 Coastal Defence Squadron, IAF Volunteer Reserve flying the Wapiti, which in 1942 became 104 (GR) Squadron IAF. The role of the flight was initially VIP transport, transport and disaster relief. In 1958 the flight received four Bell 47s and commenced a helicopter conversion training course. They were also used to support the Indian Army on reconnaissance missions and liaison flights. The flight was upgraded to a helicopter unit on 1st May 1958 and after training two Indian Navy pilots, one of the S-55s was passed onto the Navy for search and rescue duties. In the summer of 1959 a detachment was maintained at Jorhat in the North East to assist Tibetan refugees escaping over the border and this resource later became 105 HU. In 1960 they converted to the Mil-4 and moved to Hindon in March 1965. At Hindon they operated the Mil-4 and Chetak light helicopter side by side and moved onto Sarsawa in 1976. They were awarded the President Standard on 8th November 1988 and in 1990 moved to Bathinda where they re-equipped with the Mil-35 being renamed 104 Helicopter Squadron in August 1992.

Crest: *The crest depicted is that of the generic helicopter units, consisting of a rotor blade over the Himalayas and River Ganges. The squadron operations patch consists of a Firebird over a lightning strike with two crossed swords. The crossed swords signifying the army co-operation role.*

Motto: *'Stalk, Strike, Survive' 'First of the Choppers' and 'Pioneer Rotarians'.*

◀ 104 squadron Mil-35 at Bathinda in the 1990's.

Flying Squadrons 127

106 SQUADRON
'LYNX'

The squadron was raised on the 1st May 1957 on the Canberra PR57 at Agra as 106 Strategic Reconnaissance Unit. In December 1959 it merged with 102 Survey squadron with Dakotas to become 106 Strategic Reconnaissance Squadron. Its role has primarily been that of aerial reconnaissance and the unit has performed that during the conflicts of 1961, 1962, 1965, 1971 and 1999. During the Chinese conflict in 1962, the unit flew 22 missions in Akshaichin and over the Eastern frontier to confirm the build up of enemy forces. In 1965 before hostilities commenced 106 flew 30 overflights to gather information of Pakistan's intentions. During the conflict proper the units Canberras and Dakotas were kept busy over West and East Pakistan, notable missions being a long range one to Gwador Port near the Iran/Pakistan border on the 10th December 1971 and the reconnaissance mission which picked a Pakistani Armoured column approaching Longewala on 8th December 1971. Specially converted Avro 748s were inducted in 1986 which enabled the Dakotas to be retired. In the period from 1970 till 1980 the squadron embarked on a major task of photographing the whole of India, a task they did three times. Later they participated in Operation Meghdoot over the disputed Siachen Glacier, Operation Pawan over Sri Lanka between 1987 and 1989 and Operation Cactus in 1989 over the Maldives. During Operation Pawan the unit flew 543

Crest: *A Lynx.*

Motto: *'Sarva Peshayami / I See Everything'.*

Battle Honours:
Indo-Pak Conflict 1971 (West Pakistan)
Air Offensive West Pakistan
Air Offensive

▼ 106 Squadron C-47B at Agra.

hours over Sri Lanka, a fifth of which were done by the Avros which were used to carry out large scale photo mapping of the island as most road maps were over 40 years old. All IAF Canberra activities were merged into 106 squadron in August 1997 when they took over the assets of 6 squadron 'A Flight' and 35 squadron. This then gave them the additional roles of electronic warfare and target towing. Their final operational reconnaissance sorties were carried during the Kargil War of 1999. The Canberra was retired in 2007, leaving the unit to carry on with the HS-748 which was retired from the photo mapping role in December 2013. In 2014 they converted to the Su-30MKI. They were awarded the President Standard on 9th April 1975 and because of its role is the most highly decorated unit in the IAF, its aircrew having received 161 bravery awards.

▲ 106 Squadron Lynx on a Canberra at Agra in 2001.

▲ 106 Squadron Canberra TT418 at Agra in 2001.

▼ 106 Squadron Canberra PR57 performs a cartridge start at Agra in 2001.

▼ 106 Squadron Canberra with squadron badge and name at Agra.

Flying Squadrons 129

108 SQUADRON
'HAWKEYES'

Crest: *The squadron emblem portrays the bust of a Hawk mounted with a streak of lightning and a battleaxe.*

Motto: *Shodhan Aur Akraman / Search and Strike'.*

Battle Honours:
Indo-Pak Conflict 1999
Operation Safed Sagar

The Hawkeyes were formed on 20th November 1959 at Halwara on the Vampire, their role being that of army co-operation and photo reconnaissance. During the 1965 war whilst based in the East at Bagdogra they completed several photo armed reconnaissance missions and night air defence sorties. They continued to fly the Vampire until 1968 when they were re-equipped with the Su-7 at Bareilly. Operating from Halwara in the 1971 War they flew a total of 158 sorties, consisting of counter airstrikes, close air support, interdiction and tactical reconnaissance. In July 1973 they converted onto the MiG-21MF at Adampur and exchanged these for MiG-21M in October 1977, before moving back to the MF in October 1981. From 1997 until 2003 they were based at Pathankot and took part in 1999 Kargil Operations. They were forward deployed to Awantipur and tasked with strike missions in the Valley of Kaksar, Batalik, Mashkoh and Dras. They flew 152 sorties during this period of which 14 were by night. They moved to Jamnagar in 2003, taking on the MOFT role, later moving to Bhuj in 2008. They were awarded the President Standard on 22nd March 2009.

▼ Pilot in front of a 108 Squadron MiG-21M.

130 Squadrons, Patches, Heraldry & Artwork of the Indian Air Force: 1932-2016

108 Squadron

▲ 108 Squadron anniversary artwork.

◀ 108 Squadron artwork painted on a building at Jamnager.

Flying Squadrons 131

108 Squadron

▲ 108 Squadron MiG-21M's at Jamnager in 2006.

132   Squadrons, Patches, Heraldry & Artwork of the Indian Air Force: 1932-2016

125 SQUADRON
'GLADIATORS'

Formed on Mil-24 on 1st November 1983, 125 squadron were the first unit to operate the Hind in the IAF. Initially they were set up as a trials unit to develop the role of this armed platform into the IAF inventory. Their primary roles later on became anti tank, escort to heliborne ops and assault with secondary roles of SAR and troop induction. The Mil-35 was inducted into the unit in 1990 and around this time the unit was placed under the operational control of the IA. The squadron participated in Operation Pawan and was deployed to Sri Lanka for two years between October 1987 and March 1990.

Crest: A plan view of the Mil-25/35 in a sky blue roundel. Three red diamonds are placed with the roundel at 120 degree intervals signifying the three main roles of the squadron which are Anti Tank, Assault Operations and Escort to Heliborne Operations.

Motto: 'Balidaan Veerasya Bhushanam / Sacrifice is the Jewel of the Brave'.

▲ 125 Squadron Mil-35 in action at Hindon during Air Force Day.

Flying Squadrons 133

220 SQUADRON
'DESERT TIGERS'

The squadron was raised out of 51 Sqn Auxillary Air Force Squadron at Pune on 9th January 1963 with the Vampire. They were initially known at the Fighting Tigers and its role was that of operational conversion onto the Vampire for newly commissioned pilots. They moved to Pune, then Ambala and for the 1965 War they operated from Pathankot under the command of 45 squadron. The Desert Tigers converted onto the Marut in April 1969 and moved to Jodhpur in 1970. They participated in the 1971 war, operating from the forward airbase of Uttarlai, from where they performed TAC-R and CAS missions in the general area of Longewala and Chor-Dera-Maro. In all they flew 33 missions during the conflict and 68 sorties. In 1981 they moved onto the MiG-23BN and moved to Halwara to consolidate with the other MiG-23BN units in 1997. They were numberplated in 2005 and then resurrected with the Su-30MKI on 25th September 2012. They received the President's Standard on 20th November 2013.

Crest: A Tigers Head approved by the President on 2nd January 1967.

Motto: "Shauryam Tejo Dhrith / Valour Energy and Firmness".

Battle Honours:
Indo-Pak Conflict 1971 (West Pakistan)
Air Offensive West Pakistan
Air Offensive

▼ 220 Squadron MiG-23BN and crew at a gunnery detachment.

134 | Squadrons, Patches, Heraldry & Artwork of the Indian Air Force: 1932-2016

220 Squadron

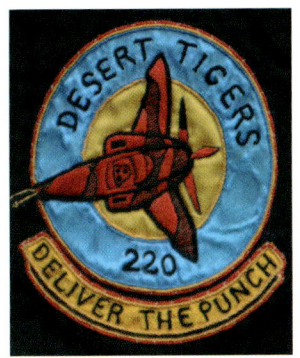

▼ 220 Squadron pilots in front of their trusty steed at Halwara.

Flying Squadrons 135

221 SQUADRON
'VALIANTS'

221 Squadron artwork outside the crew room at Halwara in 2006.

Valiants' Pilot at Halwara in 2006.

The Valiants were formed on 7th February 1963 at Barrackpore out of 55 Auxiliary Air Force Squadron. Initial equipment was the Vampire and Harvard. In February 1963 they became 221 Squadron, relocating to Kalaikunda, from where they were based during the 1965 War. In August 1968 they moved to Bareilly and converted onto the SU-7. At the start of the 1971 War, the Valiants found themselves at Panagarh having moved from Bareilly the previous October. They were allocated the tasks of CAS and TAC-R, most notably launching strikes against the airfields of Kurmitola and Tezgoan. The squadron transferred to the Western Sector on the 12th December, operating from Amritsar. They moved to Ambala in 1975, then Bathinda in 1981 and finally Halwara in February 1982 where they converted onto the MiG-23BN. In April 1984 they participated in operations over the Siachen Glacier during Operation Meghdoot. During Operation Safed Sagar over Kargil starting on 26th May 1999 the squadron struck the icy heights in the Dras Sector delivering 130 tonnes of bombs and 505 rockets, during 155 sorties. The Valiants accounted for the largest air to ground effort by any attack squadron during the six week war with Pakistan. Six of its pilots were awarded gallantry medals and the battle honour Op Safed Sagar was bestowed upon the squadron. They were the last unit to operate the MiG-23BN in the IAF, doing so until February 2009 where upon they were numberplated. Stood up on the Su-30MKI in March 2011.

Crest: *The crest depicts a distinctive and sharp triangular motif in blue and red representing a shockwave. Underneath the shockwave is a 500 kg bomb and a S-24 rocket crossed against each other. The shockwave represents its supersonic capability and the weaponry of its offensive role. The crest was adopted shortly after the conversion onto the Su-7.*

Motto: *'Tejasa Shatrun Damayah / Vanquish the Enemy With Valour'. Also use 'The Few, The Proud.'*

Battle Honours:

Indo-Pak Conflict 1971 (East Pakistan) Air Offensive for Liberation of Bangladesh   Air Offensive

Indo-Pak Conflict 1999 Operation Safed Sagar

▲ Squadron badge painted on a preserved MiG-23BN at Halwara.

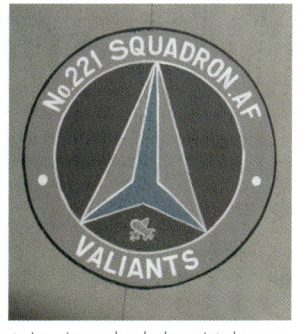

▲ Low viz squadron badge painted on a MiG-23BN at Halwara in 2006.

▲ 221 Squadron MiG-23U at Halwara in the 1980's.

Flying Squadrons   137

221 Squadron

▲ MiG-23BN and pilots at Halwara 2006.

▶ Valiant's artwork at the squadron HQ.

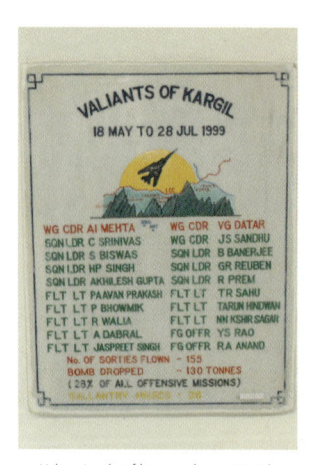

VIGILANCE OUR WATCHWORD
VICTORY OUR AIM
VIGOROUS OUR ATTACK
VALIANT OUR NAME

THE FEW - THE PROUD
THE VALIANTS

VALIANTS OF KARGIL
18 MAY TO 28 JUL 1999

WG CDR AI MEHTA	WG CDR VG DATAR
SQN LDR C SRINIVAS	WG CDR JS SANDHU
SQN LDR S BISWAS	SQN LDR B BANERJEE
SQN LDR HP SINGH	SQN LDR GR REUBEN
SQN LDR AKHILESH GUPTA	SQN LDR R PREM
FLT LT PAAVAN PRAKASH	FLT LT TR SAHU
FLT LT P BHOWMIK	FLT LT TARUN HINDWAN
FLT LT R WALIA	FLT LT NN KSHIRSAGAR
FLT LT A DABRAL	FG OFFR YS RAO
FLT LT JASPREET SINGH	FG OFFR RA ANAND

No OF SORTIES FLOWN - 155
BOMB DROPPED - 130 TONNES
(28% OF ALL OFFENSIVE MISSIONS)

▲ Valiant's role of honour during Kargil.

▶ 221 Squadron artwork 2006.

V 221
THE FEW - THE PROUD - THE VALIANTS

138 Squadrons, Patches, Heraldry & Artwork of the Indian Air Force: 1932-2016

221 Squadron

▲ Line up of 221 Squadron MiG-23BN's at Halwara in 2006, with the nearest aircraft showing of its low viz squadron logo.

▲ Night shot of a Valiants' MiG-23BN at Halwara in 2006.

Flying Squadrons 139

222 SQUADRON
'TIGERSHARKS'

The squadron was raised at Ambala on 15th September 1969 with the Su-7 and were initially called The Killers. They moved to Halwara in July 1971 and participated in the 1971 war in the western sector by launching CAS missions against Risalewala and Chander airfields. They also performed CAS missions in the Dra-Baba-Nanak, Husseinwala and Firozur sectors against enemy armour and troop concentrations. Finally they performed interdiction missions against enemy infrastructure and TAC-R deep into enemy territory. Post war they moved back to Ambala in May 1975 before moving to Hindon on 14th May 1981. They became the first IAF unit to operate the locally produced MiG-27 aircraft receiving that accolade in December 1985. Prior to moving to Hashimara on 19th May 1989, the squadron was visited by the then PM, Rajiv Gandhi who re-named them the Tigersharks.

Crest: *A MiG-27 over a Tigershark. The Tigershark symbolising the most ferocious and feared shark that has to venture far and wide in search of its prey.*

Motto: *'Vinashaya Dushkrutam / Destroyer Of Evil'.*
Also use *'Lethal At First Bite'.*

Battle Honours:
Indo-Pak Conflict 1971 (West Pakistan)
Holding Battle in Ferozpur-Fazilka
Ferozpur-Fazilka

▶ 222 Squadron pilots circa 1970's.

▶ 222 Squadron pilots circa 1980's.

140 Squadrons, Patches, Heraldry & Artwork of the Indian Air Force: 1932-2016

222 Squadron

▲ Tigersharks MiG-27 at Jodhpur in 1998.

▼ Tigersharks badge on the MiG-27.

Flying Squadrons 141

223 SQUADRON
'TRIDENTS'

Founded on 10th May 1982 on the MiG-23MF at Adampur, the unit inducted the supersonic swing fighter into the IAF and initially were known as The Swing Wing Interceptors. In the short period of MiG23MF operations they were instrumental in operating from Leh airfield at an altitude of 10,682 feet. On 27th November 1989 the unit converted onto the MiG-29 being rechristened the Tridents in 1990. During the Kargil War they flew escort missions and were awarded the battle honour of Op Safed Sagar.

▲ Squadron logo on a MiG-29A in 1997.

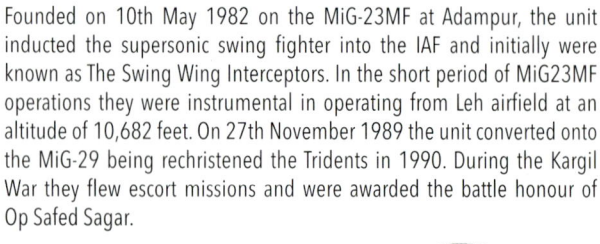

▼ Tridents MiG-29A landing at Halwara in 2006.

142 — Squadrons, Patches, Heraldry & Artwork of the Indian Air Force: 1932-2016

Crest: The unit's crest shows the striking end of the 'Varja' or 'Trident'. As per Indian Mythology, this three pronged weapon is Lord Indra's powerful Thunderbolt. The weapon was always victorious in battle and continues to be a symbol of power and speed.

Motto: 'Vijayastra Amoghastra / Weapon For Victory'.

Battle Honours:

Indo-Pak Conflict 1999
Operation Safed Sagar.

Flying Squadrons   143

224 SQUADRON
'WARLORDS'

Founded on 4th July 1983 on the MiG-23MF at Adampur from where it operated until moving to Halwara on April 9th 1996. Its prime role was that of Air Defence which it continued with up till numberplating in 2007. In between times they took part in Operation Megdoot from 1985 till 1986 and Operation Safed Sager in 1999 where they maintained a deployment of six aircraft at a forward base. On 1st September 1997 they moved to Jamnager and took on the additional role of target towing over the Sharmath Range. They were numberplated in 2007 after the retirement of the MiG-23MF, later resurrecting on the Jaguar.

▲ Warlords' Insignia on a MiG-23MF at Pune in 1998.

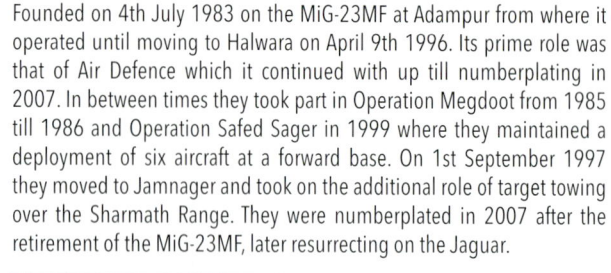

▶ Warlords' Pilots with a target sleeve after a live firing at Jamnagar.

▼ Warlords' MiG-23MF at Jamnagar.

144 Squadrons, Patches, Heraldry & Artwork of the Indian Air Force: 1932-2016

Crest: The squadron crest depicts a warrior on a chariot proceeding to war. The fearless warrior is at a state of readiness at all times with all his weapons aimed at the enemy. His strength is achieved by rigorous training, determination and dedication. The chariot signifies the weapons platform which is lethal and highly flexible, while the horses signify power and strength. The warrior and chariot combination would prove to be a deadly adversary to any enemy and thus making him a Warlord.

Motto: 'Senaninam Aham Skandhah / Among the Warriors I am the best.'

▼ Warlords' MiG-23U taxies past the squadron's hangar at Jamnagar in 1998.

Flying Squadrons 145

224 Squadron

▲ Warlords' MiG-23MF at Pune in 1998.

▼ Warlords' Pilot in front of his aircraft.

▼ Warlords' Pilots Scarf

146 Squadrons, Patches, Heraldry & Artwork of the Indian Air Force: 1932-2016

HELICOPTER UNITS

Helicopter formations in the IAF consist of squadrons, units and flights; their defining status being decided on their unit establishment. The two squadrons, 104 & 125 are included in the previous section. The number of units flying helicopters has seen three significant increases over the life of the IAF. The first in the 1960's as a result of the Chinese Aggression saw the introduction of the Mil-4 which enabled another 6 units to establish. The introduction of the Mil-8 and its successor, the Mil-17 enabled more units to form in the 1980's and 1990's and finally the receipt of the upgraded Mil-17-V5 enabled even more units to stand up, starting in 2012. For many years the crests of the Helicopter Force have standardised on one design consisting of a tail rotor over the Himalayas and the River Ganges, with an Ashoka Lion at the top and the motto *'Aapatsu Mitram/A Friend In Time Of Need'*. Occasionally some units would have different operational patches, but some units that I have visited have had nothing at all. However in the last five years, things have changed and customised unit crests have started to appear.

105 HELICOPTER UNIT
'DARING EAGLES'

Crest: An Eagle.

Motto: 'Aapatsu Mitram / A Friend In Time Of Need.'

The unit have a long and distinguished career over the skies of India having been raised in Jorhat on 23rd November 1959. Early days saw them operating with the Bell 47G and S55, later receiving two Chetaks in 1962 before converting to the Mil-4 on 30th September 1963. The first 18 years of their existence saw them operating around the demanding environs of Eastern Air Command. They saw action in the Indo-China conflict of 1962 where a three aircraft detachment at Lumpo performed reconnaissance, CASEVAC and re-supply missions in support of the Indian Army's 4th Division. Their impressive performance included the evacuation of 135 casualties from the front and the supply of 14.6 tonnes of stores. During the 1965 War the unit operated from Kumbhigram and Argatala carrying troops and supplies. The unit saw further combat during the Indo-Pak war of 1971. Noteworthy during the 1971 in the Eastern Sector was their performance at Sylhet, where together with 110 HU and 111 HU they airlifted a force of Indian Army troops across the Meghna River at night, under enemy fire. This was followed by an advance on Daudkandi and

▲ 105 HU Mil-17 at Gorakhpur in 2010.

◄ 105 HU artwork in front of their HQ Building.

148 Squadrons, Patches, Heraldry & Artwork of the Indian Air Force: 1932-2016

105 Helicopter Unit

then onto the outskirts of Dacca. The combined helicopter force completed 409 sorties in 36 nonstop hours, lifting a total of 6023 men and 5,500 kgs of supplies during the Sylhet Airlift. Throughout the conflict, 105 HU flew an impressive 94,972 kgs of supplies. They converted to the Mil-8 on 1st September 1981 and moved to their current home of Gorakhpur in August 1987. They have also taken part in various rescue missions over the decades as part of its remit to assist the civilian powers with disaster relief, predominantly with regard to floods and earthquakes. In October 1987 they were deployed to the Jaffna Peninsula in Sri Lanka to assist the Indian Army with peace keeping duties during Operation Pawan. In March 2008, they were awarded the President Standard for services to India on 25th March 2009 and in September 2010 they converted to the Mil-17.

◀ 105 HU HQ complex.

▼ 105 HU pilot, Wing Commander R.C. Pathik later went on to command the 'Sarang' display team.

Helicopter Units 149

107 HELICOPTER UNIT
'DESERT HAWKS'

Formed on the 1st June 1960 with Bell 47 and S-62 at Srinagar in Jammu & Kashmir. In 1961 they converted onto the Mil-4 and during the Indo China crisis flew extensively carrying out casualty evacuation, recce and communications flights. They moved to Bareilly in April 1965 and their helicopters were modified to carry 25 lbs bombs and a forward machine gun in the anti infiltration role during the 1965 war. They also carried out evacuation, recce, troop induction and communication flights. On 16th July 1971 they moved to Jodhpur and during the 1971 war they were again involved in the thick of battle flying 140 missions airlifting 250 passengers and 19,000 kgs of load to the forward areas. 107 HU were called upon again to operate in Sri Lanka in July 1987, being tasked with troop induction, air maintenance, communication and casualty evacuation until March 1989. In February 1991 they converted onto the Mil-8 and later the Mil-17 in February 2002. Since the last conflict the unit have been kept busy, primarily participating in the support of civil organisations during relief operations over all of India. They were awarded the President Standard on 9th March 2010.

▼ 107 HU Mil-17 at Jodhpur in 2006.

150 Squadrons, Patches, Heraldry & Artwork of the Indian Air Force: 1932-2016

Crest: *A Desert Hawk.*

Motto: *Satyamev Jayate / Truth Always Triumphs'.*

▲ Pilots of 107 HU in front of a Mil-8 in 1998.

▲ 107 HU badge on the nose of a Mil-8.

Flying Squadrons 151

109 HELICOPTER UNIT
'THE KNIGHTS'

Crest: *A Knight riding a horse with a jousting Lance.*

Motto: *'Ever Victorious'.*

The Knights were formed on 26th August 1961 at Chandigarh with the Mil-4 and participated in the 1961 Liberation of Goa and the 1962 Indo-Chinese War. In March 1965 they commenced operations from the ALG at Khanda in Gujarat from where they carried out border reconnaissance over the Rann of Kutch. On 15th August a detachment was sent to Jammu for operations prior to the 1965 war with Pakistan, where they flew with distinction in the Pathankot and Chhamb-Jaurain sectors. This detachment was moved to Srinagar for the duration of the war proper and flew 225 sorties with varied roles such as bombing, casualty evacuation, supply dropping, reconnaissance and communications. The unit moved to Kumbhigram on 1966 where they participated in operations against insurgents near the Mizo Hills and in April 1967 they moved to Jamu. During the 1971 conflict they flew 315 hours on operations and lifted out 468 casualties directly from the battle zone. On 11th January 1974 the unit converted onto the Mil-8 and moved to Hindon in 1979 from where they conducted air maintenance over the inhospitable Siachen Glacier. The unit moved to Sulur in the South on 4th June 1987 and from here participated in Operation Pawan in Sri Lanka. They were instrumental in airlifting Indian Army troops into LTTE strongholds in the Jaffna Peninsula facing ground fire on a regular basis. After Sri Lanka the unit inducted troops into the Maldives in December 1988 during Operation Cactus. They were awarded President Standard on 2nd April 1991.

▼ 109 HU Mil-8 with rocket pods at Yelahanka in 2013.

109 Helicopter Unit

▲ 109 HU Mil-8 in VIP colours. The unit maintained one helicopter in VIP configuration for duties in Southern Air Command. Taken at Yelahanka in 2001.

▶ 109 HU artwork in front of their HQ/Hangar complex.

Helicopter Units 153

110 HELICOPTER UNIT
'VANGUARDS'

'The Vanguards were formed in September 1962 at Tezpur and whilst working up on the Mil-4 were thrown into active service against the Chinese during the 1962 War. During this early period they flew to Walong ALG and one Mil-4 piloted by Flt Lt Saini received incoming small arms fire whilst on a CASEVAC mission, which damaged the helicopter. Saini was badly injured but managed to fly the helicopter to safety and for his bravery was awarded the VrC. Post war they flew operational sorties against insurgents in Mizoram and in the 1971 War, flew 409 sorties in support of the IA, including the special heliborne operation at Sylhet. Between 1973 and 1976 flood relief operations were carried out over Tripura, Manipur and Mizoram and in 1979 over Orissa. In 1981 they re-equipped with the Mil-8 and the unit was tasked with air maintenance for the IA and paramilitary forces in Nagaland, Mizoram, Tripura and Manipur. In addition they flew, CASEVAC, Communications Flights for the military and local government, VIP Flights and aid to the civil power when called upon. In 1988 110 HU participated in Operation Pawan and performed numerous missions on behalf of the IPKF. The unit continues to aid the civil power in the East and has been called on upon many times especially with regard to flood relief work. Awarded President Standard on 9th March 2011.

Crest: *Rotor blade over the Himalayas and Ganges River, with bombs and airborne supplies. The five blades of the rotor signify the strength of the unit and the multiple tasks that they perform. The background portrays their diverse area of operations from the Bay of Bengal, to the plains of the Ganges and onto the Himalayan Peaks of the Far East.*

Motto: *'Always Ahead'.*

F/O M. C. Rego and F/O K.K. Deb after landing their Mil-4 at the Tawang Helipad in December 1962 following the Indo-Chinese Border War, carrying the local tribal chief. (Photo: Air Cdr M.C. Rego)

111 HELICOPTER UNIT
'SNOW TIGERS'

Formed on 1st August 1963 with the Mil-4 at Tezpur. Initially it maintained a two aircraft detachment for use by the King of Nepal and its first major exercise was its participation in Exercise Orchid, which involved a large scale troop induction along the Burmese Border in March 1965. In August 1965 the unit moved to Srinagar in preparation for the war with Pakistan. The unit's aircraft had to be converted to use rocket pods and during the conflict used these to great effect operation out of Srinagar and Chandigarh. In January 1966 they moved back east to Hashimara and were tasked with VIP duties and air maintenance. During the 1971 war it operated in support of the IA and carried out numerous rocket attacks, CASEVAC, communications and special heliborne operations. The early seventies saw the unit give support to the local civil power and on 21st March 1976 they converted onto the Chetak. In May 1983 they moved to Bareilly and in 1986 was designated an attack unit being able to fire the ATGM. They converted onto the HAL Dhruv in 2012. Awarded the President Standard on 6th March 2012.

Crest: *A Snow Tiger with the Himalayas in the background.*

Motto: *'Aapatsu Mitram / A Friend in Time of Need'.*

◀ 111 HU Dhruv MK3 at Aero India in 2013.

Helicopter Units 155

112 HELICOPTER UNIT
'THOROUGHBREDS'

Formed on the Bell 47 on 1st August 1963 at Jorhat. In November 1966 they relocated to Bagdogra and later converted onto the HAL Chetak, remaining there until July 1982. In August 1982 they moved to Yelahanka and converted onto the Mil-8. In 1984 they came under the wing of Training Command and began to offer conversion courses on the Mil-8, continuing to present date. They participated in support of Operation Pawan and Operation Cactus. Awarded the President Standard on 11th March 2014.

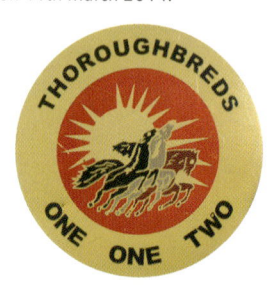

Crest: A group of thoroughbred horses over the sun. The above shows the standard HU crest of 112 HU.

Motto: 'Alma Mater of Helilift'.

◀ Close-up of the squadron badge on the nose.
▼ 112 HU Mil-8 seen at Yelahanka. Notice the *'Thoroughbreds'* nickname written around the window of the side door. 

156   Squadrons, Patches, Heraldry & Artwork of the Indian Air Force: 1932-2016

114 HELICOPTER UNIT
'SIACHEN PIONEERS'

Formed at Leh on the Chetak on 1st April 1964, it later moved to Jammu from where it maintained detachments at Srinagar and Leh. Prior to the 1965 war the unit carried out reconnaissance missions in the Srinagar sector and on behalf of the Army in the Sialkot and Uri-Poonch sectors. From September 11th until 23rd ,1965 the unit flew 105 hours in the war zone, performing reconnaissance and evacuating 79 casualties. During the 1971 war the unit was responsible for all CASEVAC, reconnaissance and communications operations in the Jammu & Kashmir sector. After the 71 war it moved to Srinagar and operated there until a move to Jammu in May 1975. In 1984 the unit became involved in Operation Meghdoot when they began to support the IA over the Siachen Glacier via air maintenance, CASEVAC and communications. During this period of intense operations they carried out the first helicopter landing on the Siachen Glacier at 15,500 feet. In August 1987 they moved back to Leh and began to operate the Cheetah, whose better performance allowed them to operate at higher helipads approaching 20,000 feet. During 1999 war in Kargil the unit was active in supporting the Indian Army. On 12th August 2009 they commenced conversion onto an up-rated version of the Cheetah known as the Cheetal. Awarded the President Standard 13th November 1996.

Crest: *Tail rotor blades over the Himalayas.*

Motto: *'Dussadhyam Kimsadhyam Kinnah / Nothing is difficult or impossible to us.'*

◀ 114 HU Cheetal at Aero India in 2013.

Helicopter Units 157

115 HELICOPTER UNIT
'HOVERING ANGELS'

Formed at Chandigarh on the 1st April 1967, flying the Mil-4. After conversion training they moved onto Jodhpur on 16th January 1968, later moving eastbound to Tezpur on 8th September 1968. On 15th September 1970 they re-equipped with the HAL Chetak at Tezpur from where they actively supported Indian Army operations during the 1971 War, maintaining detachments at Kumbhigram and Teliamura. A total of 212 sorties over 153 hours were flown in 11 days and after cessation of hostilities, they maintained a detachment at Dhaka in the newly formed Bangladesh for six months. Since then the 'Hovering Angels' have supplemented their fleet with the HAL Cheetah and have been actively involved in performing VIP Flights, communications flights, search and rescue, FAC role and aid to civil powers. Awarded the President Standard on 21st November 2014.

Crest: Front profile of a Chetak.

Motto: 'Aapatsu Mitram / A Friend in Time of Need'.

▼ 115 HU Cheetah at Tezpur in 2001.

158 ● Squadrons, Patches, Heraldry & Artwork of the Indian Air Force: 1932-2016

116 HELICOPTER UNIT
'THE TANKBUSTERS'

Formed on the 27th July 1967 on the Mil-4 at Sarsawa in the communication and casualty evacuation roles and were known as The Whirly Wizards. In December 1973 they were re-equipped with the HAL Chetak and assigned the role of anti tank operations. For this purpose the unit's helicopters were modified to carry anti tank missiles, being re-christened The Tankbusters. In 1986 they moved to Jodhpur were they have continued their role of anti tank with the addition of VIP duties and aid to civil organisations. In 1988 they sent a detachment to participate in Operation Pawan in Sri Lanka, operating from Trincomalee and Jaffna. From here they supported the Indian Army as part of the Indian Peace Keeping Force, flying offensive missile delivery missions against LTTE hideouts during which 43 missiles were launched, casualty evacuation, logistical support and armed reconnaissance. In 2012 they began conversion onto the HAL Dhruv Mk.3. Also known as the First of the Attack Choppers, they were awarded the President Standard on 5th March 2015.

Crest: Rotor blade over the Himalayas and the River Ganges.

Motto: 'Seek To Strike, Strike to Kill.'

▲ 116 HU Chetak at Jodhpur in 1999.

▲ 116 HU in grey colours at Jodhpur in 2012.

Helicopter Units   159

117 HELICOPTER UNIT
'HIMALAYAN DRAGONS'

Raised during the 1971 war on the Mil-4, it was soon baptised flying 287 sorties over 166 hours in the eastern sector. During that period they flew CASEVAC, SAR, communications and two of its aircraft were the first to land in liberated Dacca on 16th December 1971. Later they converted onto the Mil-8, followed by the Mil-17 and now the Dhruv.

Crest: A red Dragon, later replaced by a Dhruv Helicopter over a Dragon and a view of the Himalayas.

Motto: 'Shaurya Tejo Dhruti / As Brave And Bright As The Sun'.

160 Squadrons, Patches, Heraldry & Artwork of the Indian Air Force: 1932-2016

118 HELICOPTER UNIT
'CHALLENGERS'

Formed on 22nd November 1971 becoming the first unit to operate the Mil-8. They have primarily served in Eastern Air Command ever since and have undertaken many relief missions in aid to civil authorities. In 1974 the Challengers carried out SHBO into Nagaland with IA troops in order to capture hostile insurgents attempting to enter India from China. They also provided a two helicopter detachment to Sri Lanka in 1987 during Operation Pawan. In July 1994 they participated in the Orissa flood relief operations and airlifted 145,000 kgs of supplies in 9 days. They have operated from Chabua, Jorhat, Mohanbari and Guwahati in their 42 years of existence and now fly the Mil-17.

Crest: Two crossed Naga Lances above a shield.

Motto: 'Aapatsu Mitram / A Friend in Time of Need'.

Helicopter Units   161

119 HELICOPTER UNIT
"STALLIONS"

Crest: *A silhouette of a Mil-8 over a stallion's head.*

Motto: *'Ever Onward'.*

The unit were formed at Guwahati on 3rd March 1972 with the Mil-8. In October 1972 the unit was shifted to Chandigarh whereupon the unit strength was raised from 5 to 12 helicopters. In 1973 the unit participated in flood relief in Jammu & Kashmir evacuating 1400 persons in the space of 48 hours. They were relocated to Hindon in 1979 from where they carried out the air maintenance role in the north. In August 1985 they moved to Chabua in the east from where they carried out support operations for the Indian Army fighting insurgents. In support of Operation Pawan the unit moved to Sulur in February 1988 and it was here that they were christened the Stallions. They undertook extensive sorties against the LTTE during Operation Pawan, flying 3800 hours, lifting 42,026 troops and 2,820 tonnes of load. In May 1990 they moved to Jamnager and are actively engaged in support work, SAR and disaster relief. In November 2008 the unit supported the IA during Operation Black Thunder whose aim was to counter the terrorist attack in Mumbai.

▶ Early shot of Mil-8 with Stallions logo on nose.

▶ Mil-8 in later grey colour scheme at Jamnagar.

162 Squadrons, Patches, Heraldry & Artwork of the Indian Air Force: 1932-2016

121 HELICOPTER FLT
'SEA EAGLES'

The Sea Eagles operate from Mumbai civil airport with the Chetak and Mil-17-1V. They were raised in 1972 in order to support the offshore oil drilling operations of the ONGC and initially the IAF were given the responsibility of transporting off shore oil and gas workers to and from the rigs in the Arabian Sea. In 2008 the unit became involved in supporting anti terrorist attacks on the City of Mumbai by inserting commandos from the NSG into the battle area. Later the operations patch was re-designed to reflect their role in Operation Black Tornado. The gas rig in the original was moved to the sea portion of the patch and in its place on the horizon was the Mumbai skyline with NSG Commandos being lowered from the unit's Mil-17.

Crest: A Sea Eagle over the sea, showing a gas/oil rig from the Bombay High Field on the horizon. Later the operations patch was re-designed to reflect their role in Operation Black Tornado. The gas rig in the original was moved to the sea portion of the patch and in its place on the horizon was the Mumbai skyline with NSG Commandos being lowered from the unit's Mil-17.

Motto: 'Aapatsu Mitram / A Friend in Time of Need'.

▲ 121 HF Chetak at Pune in 1996. At the time this helicopter was the oldest Chetak in service.

▲ 121 HF Mil-17 over Mumbai.

Helicopter Units   163

122 HELICOPTER FLT
'FLYING DOLPHINS'

Formed on 26th September 1981 on the Mil-8 at Kalaikunda, their main roles being that of VIP transport and SAR. They moved to Port Blair on 1st April 1985 in the Andaman and Nicobar Group of Islands and have remained there ever since providing inter island communications, SAR, VIP transport, surveillance and troop induction. During the December 2004 Asian Tsunami, they performed admirably, rescuing 350 persons on the first day of the disaster.

Crest: Two Dolphins leaping out of the sea. The Dolphins being abundant in the Bay of Bengal in which the Andaman and Nicobar group of islands sit.

Motto: 'First Overseas'.

▲ 122HF Mil-8 over the seas surrounding the Car Nicobar Islands.

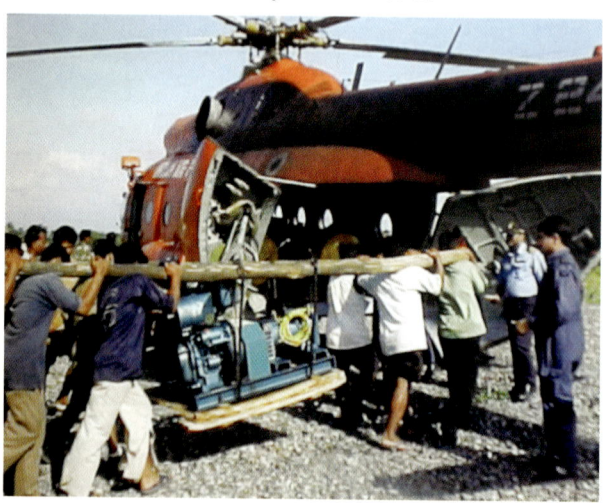

▲ 122HF Mil-8 during Tsunami relief work in 2004.

164 Squadrons, Patches, Heraldry & Artwork of the Indian Air Force: 1932-2016

126 HELICOPTER FLT
'FEATHERWEIGHTS'

Raised at Chandigarh on 15th May 1986, the Featherweights started operations with two heavy lifting Mil-26. In September 1986 whilst on a supply mission, a Mil-26 landed at Daulat Beg Oldi (DBO) which is only 8 kms from the line of actual control with China and at 16,614 ft is the world's highest operational airfield. Their heavy lift capabilities have also been utilized in the East of the country where they transported Indian Army field guns and road construction equipment into Hayuliang, which is very close to the borders with China and Burma. Other oversize cargo has included unserviceable Mil-8 helicopters and complete hospital containers which were airlifted into Thoise. In 1989 another two Mil-26's were received enabling the unit to utilize all of the air landing grounds in Jammu & Kashmir and Arunachal Pradesh.

Crest: A profile view of the Mil-26.

Motto: 'Magnus Valious / Heaviest & Mightiest'.

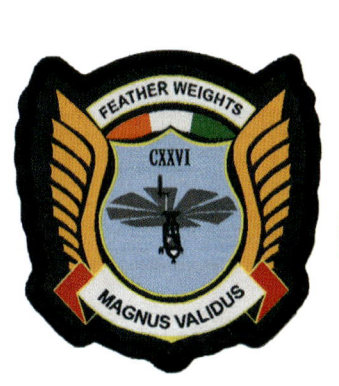

▼ One of the unit's Mil-26 in action in 2008.

Helicopter Units 165

127 HELICOPTER UNIT
'FIRST OF THE RANAS'

Raised on the 10th January 1985 at Hindon, the unit was the first to receive the Mil-17, which was to become known as the Rana in IAF Service, leading to them being christened the First of The Ranas. The term Rana meaning a historical title of Rajput origin denoting absolute Monarch Their first commander was Wg Cdr Fali Homi Major who later went on to command the IAF. On 21st August 1987 the unit moved to Chabua and later onto Mohanbari in June 1992. During the 28 years of their existence the unit have participated in major operations all over India, including numerous relief aid to the local governments. From their base in Assam they have also actively assisted the Border Roads Task Force in the construction of new roads to the far flung areas of Arunachal Pradesh by ferrying in 25 disassembled bulldozers in underslung mode. The First Ranas have also seen their fair share of active service having participated in Operations Vijay, Rhino, Pawan, Rakshak, Meghddot, Brasstack and Safed Sagar.

Crest: *Head on view of a Mil-17 in a triangle.*

Motto: *'Undaunted & Undeterred'.*

▲ The 'First of the Ranas' crew room in 2001.

▶ 127 HU Mil-17 in old green colours in 2001.

166 Squadrons, Patches, Heraldry & Artwork of the Indian Air Force: 1932-2016

128 HELICOPTER UNIT
'SIACHEN TIGERS'

The Siachen Tigers were formed on 30th December 1985 at Hindon, becoming the second unit stood up to specifically operate the Mil-17. Soon after forming they moved to operate in the heights around the Siachen Glacier where they flew over 2000 hours and lifted 200 tonnes of load and passengers. They flew actively during IPKF Operations in Sri Lanka in 1987 under Operation Pawan and Operation Rakshak in J&K against insurgents during 1990-91. In March 1988 they moved over to Eastern Air Command, initially at Chabua before moving onto their current home at Mohanbari in May 1992. Their peace time role is to support the Government of Arunachal Pradesh, the IA and the BRTF by means of air logistical support, CASEVAC, disaster relief and communications. In times of conflict they will provide support to heliborne operations, armament delivery and air logistical support. They formed a vital part of operations from Srinagar during Safed Sagar over the Kargil Peaks flying a total of 62 sorties during which 224 battle casualties were evacuated. In its peacetime role the unit have participated in flood relief operations in 1988, 1991, 2000 and 2001. As part of its support to the BRTF the unit has moved 24 bulldozers, 4 trucks, one roller and 9 air compressors as underslung loads during the period 2001-2.

Crest: A Mil-17 and Trident over the Himalayas.

Motto: 'Aapatsu Mitram / A Friend in Time of Need.'

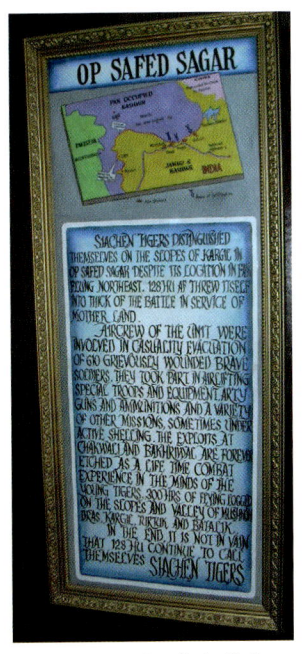

▲ Commemorative board in the 'Siachen Tigers' crew room describing their feats during Operation Safed Sagar.

Helicopter Units 167

129 HELICOPTER UNIT
'NUBRAWARRIORS'

Crest: A warrior's double edged sword with lightening emanating from it, above which is a warrior's golden helmet and below are the numerals '129'. The name Nubrawarriors was taken from the River Nubra which flows out of the Siachen Glacier.

Motto: 'Never Give In.' Also used are 'Indomitables' and 'Sri Lanka to Siachen'.

Battle Honours:
Indo-Pak Conflict 1999
Operation Safed Sagar

The unit was raised at Hindon in July 1987 with the Mil-17. Within six days of forming they provided five helicopters to participate in Operation Pawan in Sri Lanka, where they flew 877 hours airlifting 11,829 passengers and 613 tonnes of load. Immediately after returning from Sri Lanka they were deployed to Thoise in the Siachen Glacier to participate in Operation Meghdoot. Operating in the demanding environment of this rugged terrain they lifted 393 tonnes of load in just nine days. In 1988 the unit became the first Mil-17 unit in the IAF to undertake the armament role with 57mm rockets. Since then they have participated flood relief operations in 1987, 1988 and 1998 plus counter terrorism operations in the Punjab in July 1988. In May 1999 the unit deployed to Srinagar to take part in Operation Safed Sagar from where attack missions were flown against enemy strongholds on the high points over Kargil. Unfortunately one helicopter and its crew were lost to a Pakistani fired missile on 28th May 1999 forcing a reassessment of helicopter activity in that hostile environment.

▶ 129 HU Mil-17 seen on display at Palam.

Squadrons, Patches, Heraldry & Artwork of the Indian Air Force: 1932-2016

130 HELICOPTER UNIT
'CONDORS'

Formed on 15th February 1988 at Jammu with the Mil-17, the Condors main operating area has been the snow bound areas of Kashmir and Laddakh where they have supported the IA with a dedicated medium lift capability. During Operation Meghdoot, they perform the role of logistical support to Army units in and around the Siachen Glacier primarily by para dropping. Between 1990-91 they performed numerous counter insurgency operations on behalf of the Indian Army in J&K during exercise Rakshak. They participated in Operation Safed Sagar in 1999 and flew 215 hours and lifting 715 tonnes of load. They converted to the improved Mil-17-1V in February 2001.

Crest: The unit crest depicts the largest living bird in the world, i.e. The Condor.

Motto: 'We support Life'. Signifying the dependence on them of the IA whose lifeline depends on the air effort.

Battle Honours:

Indo-Pak Conflict 1999
Operation Safed Sagar

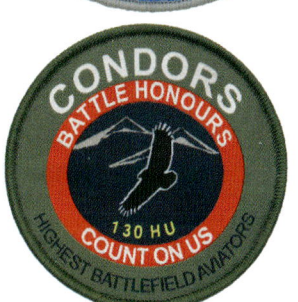

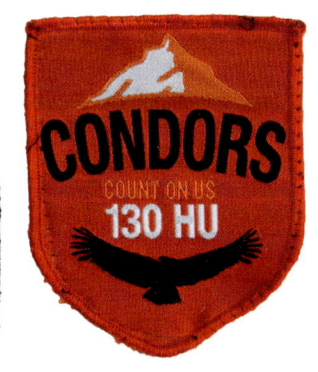

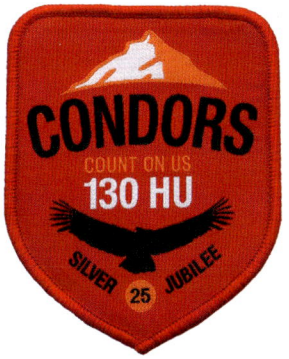

Helicopter Units   169

131 FAC FLT
'AIRBORNE POINTERS'

Formed on 2nd August 1974 at Pathankot, becoming the IAF's first Forward Air Control Flight, whose role it is to assist fighter aircraft to track their targets. The flight was initially equipped with six Bell 47G helicopters, it later moving to Udhampur in September 1975 and re-equipping in 1980 with the Cheetah. They moved to Leh to operate over the Siachen Glacier, before moving to Halwara in July 1987 and then Hindon in March 1996, where it merged with 134 FAC Flight (Airwolves). Later the unit took on some HAL Chetak helicopters and continues with both types.

Crest: A head on view of a Cheetah Helicopter in a circle with a blue surround containing the units name. Later changed to a side on view of a Cheetah over an Eagle's Head.

Motto: 'Savage And Powerful'. Also uses the sayings, 'Eagle Eyes' and 'Search to Guide.'

▼ 131 Fac Flt Cheetah over Halwara in 2008.

170   Squadrons, Patches, Heraldry & Artwork of the Indian Air Force: 1932-2016

132 FAC FLT
'HOVERING HAWKS'

Formed on 24th February 1986 with HAL Cheetah at Udahampur. Its main role was to provide airborne FAC support to the fighter aircraft of the IAF in the Jammu & Kashmir sector. In October 1997, 135 FAC Flight was merged into the unit. The unit has participated in Operations Meghdoot, Rakshak and Safed Sagar. During Safed Sagar the unit maintained a four helicopter detachment at Srinagar during which they flew airborne FAC, Recce, communications, SAR and CASEVAC. The flight flew 395 missions and in doing so became the first IAF unit to perform the airborne FAC role in the tactical battle area and five of their pilots were awarded gallantry awards. Currently the flight operates the Cheetah and Chetak helicopters and maintains a flight at Khalsi, from where Army posts at 16,500 feet are air maintained and a detachment at Srinigar for SAR and communications duties.

Crest: A Cheetah with the backdrop of a rising sun and a Hovering Hawk.

Motto: 'Savage And Powerful'.

▼ 132 FAC Flight Cheetah over J&K.

Helicopter Units 171

141 SSS FLT
'FLAMINGOS'

Formed in 1974 with Mil-4 at Jamnager; the unit perform SAR missions over the Rann of Kutch. They converted onto the Chetak in August 1981. The Flamingoes have given aid to the local government during natural disasters and they supplied two aircraft to support the de-induction of the IPKF from Sri Lanka in 1990. They maintain detachments at several airbases in the SWAC.

Crest: *A Flamingo flying over the Arabian Sea as the sun rises.*

Motto: *'Aaptsu Mitran / A Friend In Time Of Need.'*

▲ Below: Head on view of a 141 SS FLT Chetak with floats.

▼ Bottom: 141 SS FLT Chetak airborne over the Rann of Kutch.

172 — Squadrons, Patches, Heraldry & Artwork of the Indian Air Force: 1932-2016

142 SSS FLT
"FLYING AMPHIBS"

Formed on 1st August 1974, they currently operate the Cheetah and Chetak.

Crest: A Cheetah over the Himalayas on top of a float equipped Chetak over the sea.

Motto: 'Sea to Summit'.

Helicopter Units 173

151 HELICOPTER UNIT
'SARANG'

The Sarang Helicopter Display Team were formed on the Indigenous HAL Dhruv on March 18 2002 at Bangalore. The unit's role was to showcase the professionalism of the IAF and to demonstrate the ability of the Indian Aviation Industry in developing their own range of helicopters. Their debut performance was in Singapore during Asian Aerospace in 2004. Since then it has performed at many events in India and around the world. They moved to Yelahanka in April 2005 and then to Sulur in November 2009.

Crest: A Peacock. (Sanskrit translation of which is Sarang).

Motto: 'Fly The Best'.

▼ Sarang Team at Aero India in 2015.

174 Squadrons, Patches, Heraldry & Artwork of the Indian Air Force: 1932-2016

151 Helicopter Unit

▲ Sarang Team in formation at Aero India in 2011.

Helicopter Units   175

152 HELICOPTER UNIT
'MIGHTY ARMOUR'

Formed on the 14th September 1988 with Mil-17. They have provided relief operations several times including the Bhuj earthquake in 2001 and Patna flood relief in 2004. They converted onto the Mil-17-1V in May 2001. The unit participated over Kargil during Operation Safed Sagar operating from the Srinagar Valley with a detachment of 5 helicopters. Their missile attack mission on the 26th May over Tololing and Tiger Hill was the first attack mission carried out by the IAF during the war. Five offensive missions were carried out over the next two days before the role of attack helicopters at such high altitude was re-assessed. The unit changed onto air supply missions and CASEVAC missions on behalf, resulting in the succesfull evacuation of 207 casualties. Over the period they flew 411 sorties and clocked up 160 hours. From the end of 2009 until 2011 the unit maintained a five helicopter detachment at Jagdalpur in support of IA Operations against Naxalites insurgents.

Crest: Armour, swords and shield over a blue and yellow shield.

Motto: 'Who Dares Wins.'

Battle Honours:
Indo-Pak Conflict 1999
Operation Safed Sagar.

153 HELICOPTER UNIT
'DARING DRAGONS'

Formed on the 1st November 1988 with Mil-17 at Udhampur. The main task of the unit has been to provide the task of air maintenance to IA units in and around the Siachen Glacier and within months of formation they were participating in Operation Meghdoot. Since inception they have provide support to heliborne operations, air maintenance, CASEVAC and para dropping. They were detached to Sri Lanka in May 1989 during Operation Pawan where they were involved with attack missions against the LTTE from their base at Vavuniya.

Crest: *A Mil-17 above a snow covered peak of the Himalayas, flanked by two Ladakhi Dragons. The Dragon being the symbol of strength and power.*

Motto: *'The Invincibles'.*

◀ A Daring Dragon Mil-17 over J&K.

Helicopter Units   177

154 HELICOPTER UNIT
'SNOW LEOPARDS'

Raised on the Mil-17-V5.

Crest: A Snow Leopard over the Himalayan Peaks.

Motto: 'Victory, Valour'.

155 HELICOPTER UNIT
'KRIPANS'

First Unit to be inducted on the Mil-17-V5 in February 2012.

Crest: The crest depicts a Kripan which is a Sikh Sword.

Motto: "First into the Future / Committed to Excellence'.

Squadrons, Patches, Heraldry & Artwork of the Indian Air Force: 1932-2016

156 HELICOPTER UNIT
'ARMOURED KESTRELS'

Raised on the Mil-17-V5.

Crest: A Kestrel superimposed over the Himalayan Mountains and River.

Motto: 'Versatility and Valour'.

157 HELICOPTER UNIT
'TARKSHYA'

The fourth unit to be raised on the Mil-17-V5 in June 2013.

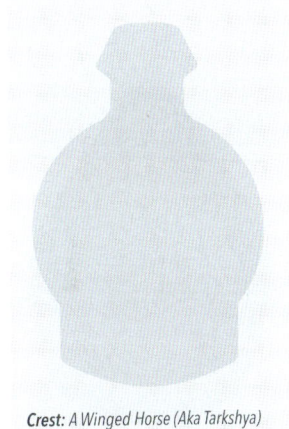

Crest: A Winged Horse (Aka Tarkshya) over day/night signifying 24 hour capability.

Motto: 'Virtuous, Valiant, Victorious'.

◀ Mil-17-V5 at Aero India in 2015.

Helicopter Units   179

158 HELICOPTER UNIT
'SILVER FALCHIONS'

Raised on the Mil-17-V5.

Crest: A Falchion is a one handed single edged sword.

Motto: 'Victory Bestows on the Virtuous'

159 HELICOPTER UNIT
'FLYING DAGGERS'

Raised on the Mil-17-V5.

Crest: -

Motto: -

▲ Mil-17-V5 inbound to Yelahanka for Aero India in 2013.

180 Squadrons, Patches, Heraldry & Artwork of the Indian Air Force: 1932-2016

United Nations Missions

IAF SQUADRON 2000

A contingent of IAF assets was sent to Sierra Leone in 2000 as part of the United Nations Mission. The IAF force initially consisted of four Mil-8's and four Chetaks which were despatched in May. As the situation on the ground deteriorated these were joined on the 2nd June by three Mil-35's at Kenema. Operation Kukri was instigated to rescue 222 peacekeepers held hostage by the RUF Rebels and over four days IAF 2000 flew 98 sorties. The Chetaks were used in the airborne command and CASEVAC roles, whilst the Mil-8's were used for troop carrying and supplies and the Mil-35's for ground attack and convoy escort duties.

▲ Mil-17 belonging to IAF Squadron 2000.

▼ Mil-35 at Kenema after Operation Kukri.

Helicopter Units 181

United Nations Missions

IAF SQUADRON 2003
'THE VIPERS'

The squadron was set up on 1st August 2003 as a sub component of the Indian Aviation Contingent number 1 (IAC-1) which was part of the Indian Peace Keeping effort in the Congo. IAF squadron 2003 was equipped with 4 Mil-25 helicopters at Goma and the New Dromo Camp in Bunia. They were the cutting edge of the IAF effort in the Congo and roles included armed recce, fire support for heliborne forces and escort to UN vehicles and ground forces. The unit had flown over 6,000 flight hours till the time they were de-inducted on 15th October 2010.

IAF SQUADRON 2005
'THE FIREBIRDS'

The squadron was raised on 4th February 2005 with a fleet of four Mil-35's and together with IAF Squadron 2006, formed the Indian Aviation Contingent II (IAC-II). They were based at Goma alongside the assets of IAC-1. The Mil-35 helicopters with their night fighting capability were to be drawn from 104 Helicopter Squadron, the oldest helicopter unit in the IAF and the first to be deployed overseas as a unit. They operated in the attack and armed reconnaissance role and by the 30th July 2010 had completed over 4,000 hours of accident free flying.

IAF SQUADRON 2006
'THE KIVU HAWKS'

Inducted on 4th February 2005, the Kivu Hawks flew the Mil-17 from Bukavu. The unit like Squadrons 2003 and 2004 had crews drawn from many IAF squadrons and helicopter units. Their main role was that of logistics and by July 2010 had completed over 11,500 sorties and more than 7,000 hours of flying.

IAF SQUADRON 2004
'THE EQUATORIAL EAGLES'

The second component of IAC-1 was formed on 21st July 2003 with five Mil-17 helicopters tasked with logistics, troop insertion/extraction, casualty evacuation, search and rescue and reconnaissance. They flew over 13,000 sorties and 8,000 flight hours until de-induction on 15th October 2010. For the good work carried out by the unit, they were awarded a unit citation by the UN force commander.

UN MISSION SUDAN
'NILE WARRIORS'

The IAF mission to Sudan was the first military aviation contingent to deploy as part of the UN Mission in Sudan. They arrived at Kadugli Airport with their Mil-17's in October 2005 and withdrew on 27th December 2010. In that period, 5 contingents from the IAF participated, flying a total of 10,420 hours, carrying 1,435,814 kgs of cargo and 71,814 passengers.

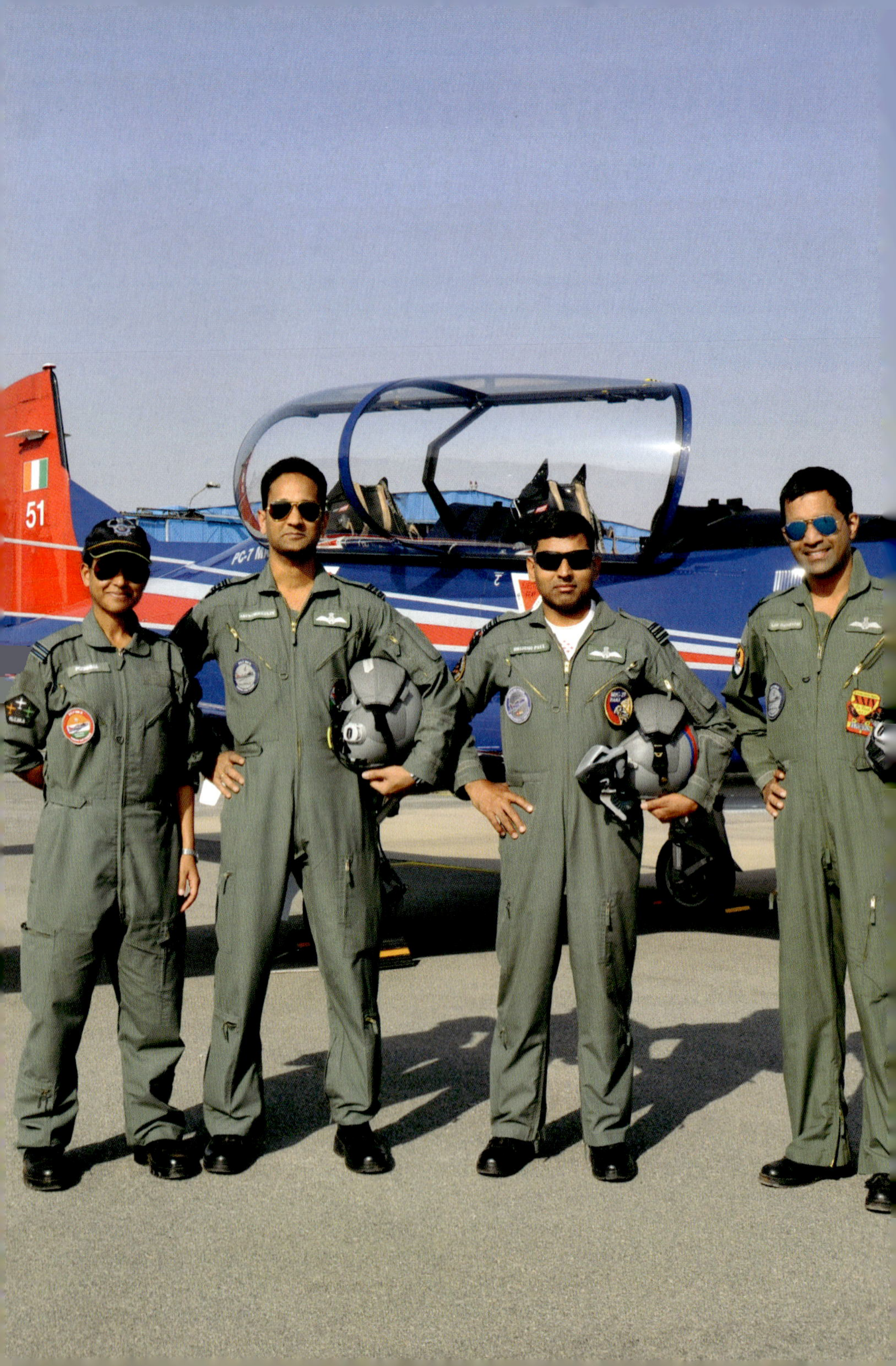
51

NON NUMBERED FLYING UNITS

There are approximately 30 non numbered units that have operated aircraft in the IAF, including several that have seen combat.

AIRCRAFT AND SYSTEMS TESTING ESTABLISHMENT

Crest: *The crest shows a futuristic aircraft carrying guided weapons ringed by an ellipse. The slide rule superimposed on the aircraft portrays the precision and accuracy needed for flight testing. The missile signifies armament that forms the major preoccupation of ASTE. The ring depicts the sighting ring of the gunsight which symbolizes the involvement of ASTE with armament and the constant vigil for correct aims and objectives.*

Motto: *'Sukshamta Avum Utkarsh / Precision and Excellence'.*

▼ ASTE Badge on a Kiran MK1 at Bangalore in 2003.

The Aircraft and Systems Testing Establishment (ASTE) was founded in 1972 at the Indian Air Force's No 1 Base Repair Depot in Kanpur. The unit can trace its origins back to the Aircraft and Armament Testing Unit (AATU), which was initially established at Kanpur in April 1957 to flight test the Folland Gnat, which India was interested in purchasing and manufacturing. At the time of its origin in 1957, the AATU consisted of 2 officers, 6 senior non-commissioned officers and 31 other ranks. It received its first aircraft on 8th September 1957, when a Dassault Mystere IV arrived for Aden Ammunition trials with the DEFA 30mm gun. For the next two years they worked on the Hunter, Mystere IVA and Gnat. A fairly quiet period proceeded thereafter with many pilots being posted back to operational squadrons, until the next major task for the unit arrived in 1964, in the shape of the Marut Jet Fighter which was the first jet fighter designed and manufactured in India under a design team headed by Dr Kurt Tank. A team of three test pilots and two engineers arrived at the HAL Plant in Bangalore during March 1964 to commence trials. Simultaneously another HAL Product, the Krishak, a single engined observation aircraft, was being tested at Kanpur, Bangalore and in the remote Northeast at Misamari, home of the first Army AOP unit to receive the type. The threat of war with Pakistan during September 1965 put the unit under severe pressure. At one point 20 different tasks were underway at the AATU, including Napalm bomb release for the Mystere IVA and gun improvements for the Gnat. After the 65 war new types were received from HAL for testing including the Kiran jet trainer and Chetak. By 1967, the Marut and the Kiran trials were the major projects in house

▲ ASTE Kiran MK1 in 2003.

186   Squadrons, Patches, Heraldry & Artwork of the Indian Air Force: 1932-2016

Aircraft and Systems Testing Establishment

▲ ASTE Chetak at Yelahanka 1996.

at the AATU. Working closely with HAL, the unit was able to improve both products with a list of recommended modifications. Trials were taking place on all manner of items and with this widening role, the AATU metamorphosed into ASTE on 23rd August 1972 and completed a move to Bangalore in June 1973. The main ASTE activities were to be linked with HAL, the Defence Research and Development Organisation (DRDO), the IAF, Army and Navy. Projects were to include weapons, airborne systems, avionics, ground-based radar's, simulators and aircraft. In July 1973, ASTE set up its own test pilots school in order to train Production Test Pilots to carry out test flights on production aircraft and overhauled aircraft at HAL and IAF repair facilities. The first Indian Experimental Test Pilots Course was initiated in September 1976. Following problems with the Marut activities on domestic aircraft design and development slowed and as a consequence the emphasis shifted to the integration of weapons of western origin onto Russian Aircraft and vice versa. For instance the

◀ A close up of the ASTE Badge on a Chetak.

Non Numbered Flying Units 187

Aircraft and Systems Testing Establishment

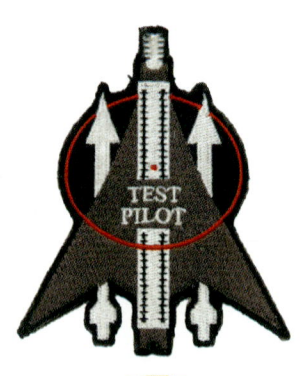

▲ ASTE An-32 at Bangalore in 2003.

R550 Magic air to air missiles (AAM) were integrated onto the MiG-21BIS fitted with a Smiths Head up Display. Others included Russian 57mm UB57-16 rocket pods fitted to the Gnat derivative known as the Ajeet, Russian R60 AAM's fitted to the Hunter and S24 heavy calibre unguided rockets onto the Canberra. Between 1975 and 1980 indigenous armaments and avionics equipment became available for trials with a view for fitment onto the existing IAF Fleet. Also development work on fixed wing aircraft resurrected itself in the late 70's with the introduction of the HPT-32 trainer. During the 1970/80's ASTE pilots made several visits to Europe and the Soviet Union to test types such as the Jaguar, Buccaneer, Mirage series, Viggen, MiG-23 and MiG-27. When the Jaguar was selected for the deep penetration strike aircraft the workload at ASTE was to increase drastically as the platform was integrated into the fleet. ASTE became involved with development trials on advanced avionics, communications and armaments, resulting in an expansion to meet the need. In 1984, two Test Pilots from ASTE were selected to undergo training for the planned Indo-Soviet Joint Space Venture. One of these men, Squadron Leader Rakesh Sharma, became the first Indian in space when he was launched on 3rd April 1984 onboard a Soyuz T11 spacecraft. Further overseas evaluations took place on the MiG-29, Mil-26, Mil-17, Dornier 228 and Chinook, and with the arrival of the IL-78 into the fleet, flight-refuelling procedures had to be developed to service the Jaguar, Mirage, MiG-27 and Su-30. ASTE Test Pilots have been and continue to be involved with the development of the Su-30 and MiG-21UPG in India and Russia. Flight testing currently continues on three of HAL's major new projects; the Advanced Light Helicopter (Dhruv), Light Combat Aircraft (Tejas) and the HAL HJT36 Intermediate Jet Trainer. A combined test force has been set up to test the Dhruv for the IAF, Navy and Army, under the control of ASTE. The current fleet of ASTE consists of HS-748, An-32, MiG-21UM, MiG-21UPG, Jaguar M/IS/IT, Kiran, Cheetak, Mil-8, Mirage 2000 and Su-30. To date ASTE and its predecessor have completed over 900 trials and also over 150 fixed and rotary wing Test Pilots (including one Iraqi) and 62 Flight Test Engineers have graduated from the course set up originally in 1973. President Standard awarded on 21st November 2005.

Aircraft and Systems Testing Establishment

▲ The NAL Saras ("Crane") is the first Indian multi-purpose civilian aircraft in the light transport aircraft category as designed by the National Aerospace Laboratories (NAL).

▼ The recently formed IAF Historical Flight uses a Tiger Moth and Harvard from Hindon crewed by Test Pilots from ASTE. Pictured at Aero India in 2013.

Non Numbered Flying Units   189

AIRCREW EXAMINATION BOARD

The AEB was established at Palam in July 1951 as the Aircrew Training & Testing Team and their initial equipment was a Dakota, later joined by a Dove and Vampire T55. They had responsibility for testing transport pilots on long range navigation, instrument flying for fast jet pilots and visiting academies in order to check the qualified flying instructors. Later re-christened as the AEB, it moved to Hindon in March 1965. The aim of the AEB is to maintain a high standard of professional knowledge and skill of aircrew. In May 1969, Delta Flight was added to the board with the added responsibility of inspecting the helicopter stream. Currently the AEB performs quality audits on all aircrew within the IAF, achieving this by pilot categorisation, instrument ratings and standardisation. Awarded the President's Standard on 1st November 2004.

Crest: A compass over a Himalayan Eagle atop an open textbook.

Motto: 'Dhee Kaushalam Poornata / Knowledge, Merit and Perfection'.

AIR DEFENCE FLIGHT

The Air Defence Flight was formed at Jodhpur on 15th September 1958 as the Control and Reporting School. Their initial equipment was the Vampire and they were tasked with training fighter controllers. During the 1971 war they were temporarily given the unit designation of 121 squadron for operations. In October 1972 they moved to Bakshi Ka Talab, near Lucknow and there the Vampires gave way to the HAL Marut in 1975. The flight became known as the Radar Flight and later the Marut Flight. The C&R School was upgraded to an Air Defence College on 15th March 1980, and conducted courses for fighter controllers and senior sector controllers. The Marut was retired from the flight on 31st March 1983 and the unit converted to MiG-21M. The flight became independent from the College becoming known as the Air Defence Flight. They played a supporting role to the Air Defence College in nearby Lucknow, specifically to give practice intercepts to trainee ground controllers in the art of control and reporting. The Air Defence Flight was numberplated in 2006 and its activities taken over by 35 squadron, who moved in from Bareilly.

Crest: *Himalayan Eagle holding a lightning bolt over an oil lamp. The Eagle being representing the IAF and the oil lamp reflecting the college's status as a seat of learning.*

Motto: *'Rakshyanaya Sikshaamaha / Teaching the Virtue of Defence'.*

◀ The ADF Nameboard at BKT.

▼ Maruts of the ADF in the early 1980's.

Non Numbered Flying Units 191

AIR FORCE ACADEMY

Badge: *The AFA crest shows a Himalayan Eagle perched on top of an oil lamp which represents the institutions stature as a seat of learning. The Eagle being a symbol of the IAF.*

Motto: *'Shram se Siddhi / Achievement through Diligence'.*

▲ AFA Crest on a Kiran Mk1 at Bidar in 1998.

The AFA was founded at Dundigal on 16th January 1971 following the amalgamation of two training institutions, namely No 1 Air Force College and No 2 Air Force College. No 1 Air Force College traces its origins back to No 1 (Indian) Service Flying Training School which was raised at Ambala on 1st November 1940 with the Tiger Moth and Harvard. This unit was disbanded on 1st april 1946 and in mid 1947, following partition, 151 OTU and Spitfire Flight arrived from Peshawar bringing with a mixture of types including the Spitfire Mk.VIIIe, Spitfire Mk.XIV, Harvard, Hurricane and Vengeance TT1. These were merged into 1 SFTS in August 1947 and re-named as the Advanced Flying School (India). On 28th October 1947, two Spitfire Mk.VIIIe's and a Harvard from the AFS were used in the defence of Srinagar during the Kashmir War. They deployed to Srinagar Airfield and attacked enemy vehicles and troop formations, later being joined by more aircraft from the AFS on the 30th. The Spitfire Mk.VIIIe could operate on the narrow runway at Srinagar, whilst the Spitfire Mk.XIV from the front line squadrons could not because of their width. The detachment became for a short while, No 1 (Ad Hoc) squadron and offensive action continued into December 1947. In August 1949 the school was raised to the status of academy and henceforth became known as No 1 AFA. At this point the remaining Spitfires which had been joined by several Tempest II's formed into the Conversion Training Unit and received ten Spitfire T Mk.IX tandem trainers. No 1 AFA due to the lack of space at Ambala was moved to Begumpet near Hyderabad in October 1951 and the CTU was moved to Hakimpet. In August 1955, No 1 AFA, by then flying the Harvard, was renamed as No 1 Air Force College. No 2 Elementary Flying School at Jodhpur was run by the RAF from 1941 until 1947 using the Tiger Moth,

▲ Kiran Mk2 at Hakimpet in 2001.

Cornell and Harvard. The Cornell's were retired due to severe problems with their wooden frames and the Percival Prentice was introduced in 1950 lasting until 1956. Renamed No 2 Air Force Academy in 1951, it became No 2 Air Force College in 1955. On 10th January 1955 the HAL HT2 was inducted into the unit. No 2 AFC remained at Jodhpur with the Harvard/T-6, until 1971 when it merged with No 1 Air Force College to become the AFA. In January 1974 the HAL Kiran was introduced which allowed the Harvard to be phased out in late 1975. In July 1985, the HAL HPT-32 was introduced for basic ab initio and a stage 2 advanced jet training course was introduced in July 1988. This advanced stage 2 was moved to the out station at Hakimpet in January 2006 leaving the Academy to concentrate on stage 1 of flying training. The AFA received the President Standard on 10th September 1975 and was the first non operational unit to do so. The HPT-32 was retired in 2013 and replaced by the Pilatus PC-7 MK.II.

▲ AFA Kiran MK1 gets airborne at Bidar in 1998.

▲ Original 1940 SFTS badge.

▶ Early Crests of No's 1 & 2 AFA.

Non Numbered Flying Units   193

Air Force Academy

▲ The first PC-7 MK.II for the IAF at Aero India 2013.

194 Squadrons, Patches, Heraldry & Artwork of the Indian Air Force: 1932-2016

AIR FORCE STATION BIDAR

AFS Bidar is part of the Training Command group of four airfields around Hyderabad that concentrate on the training of pilots. Initially in 1963, No 2 Jet Training Wing (JTW) was set up flying the Vampire. The station was temporarily closed in 1965, returning to service in 1966 when the Pilot Training establishment moved in with HAL HT2's from Allahabad, rechristening as the Elementary Flying School (EFS). In 1985, the EFS was renamed AFS Bidar and in June 1988, the HAL Kiran MK.II was inducted offering stage 2 (advanced) training. Later in January 2006 they started to offer stage 3 flying training on the Kiran. This was then replaced by the Hawk Operational Training Squadron (HOTS) in 2007 initially with one squadron known as 'A'. As Hawk deliveries increased, so 'B', 'C' and later 'D' squadrons were set up, with two moving out to Kalaikunda in 2014. (See HOTS page 214).

Badge: The crest depicts two Eagles ready to pounce on their pray.

Motto: 'Rakshnay Prashikshanam / Training for Defence'.

▼ A Hawk Mk.132 from HOTS at Yelahanka in 2003.

Non Numbered Flying Units   195

AIR FORCE STATION HAKIMPET

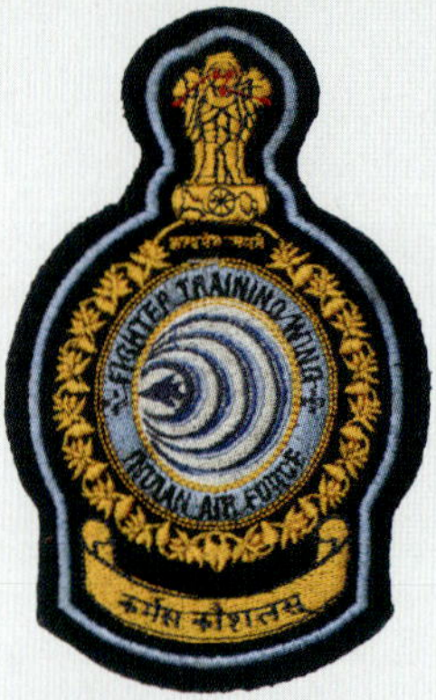

This station, in the group of training command airfields around Hyderabad started life as the Conversion Training Unit in 1951, equipped with the Tempest and Spitfire. It was renamed as the Jet Training Wing with Vampires in 1958, becoming the Fighter Training Wing in 1964 and AFS Hakimpet in 1983. In 1975 the Vampires were replaced by the Kiran and later augmented by the Iskra. In both the 1965 and 1971 wars with Pakistan, the FTW raised an operational unit (as 121 ad hoc Squadron) using the instructors in order to support the frontline IAF squadrons. The Iskra was retired on 16th December 2004, leaving the Kiran in service.

Badge: The crest depicts the compressibility of air due to the effects of an aircraft in flight.

Motto: 'Karmasu Kaushalam / Work With Excellence'.

▲ Line up of Iskras at Hakimpet in 2001.
▼ Nose of an Iskra showing the Hakimpet Crest.

▶ Welcoming board outside AFS Hakimpet.

196   Squadrons, Patches, Heraldry & Artwork of the Indian Air Force: 1932-2016

AIR FORCE TECHNICAL COLLEGE, TETTRA, TECHNICAL FLIGHTS AND BASE REPAIR DEPOTS (BRD)

Crest: *The AFTC Crest depicts a torch which symbolises learning, with streaks of lightening.*

Motto: *'Gyanen Shoba Mahey / It is through knowledge that we find pride in ourselves'.*

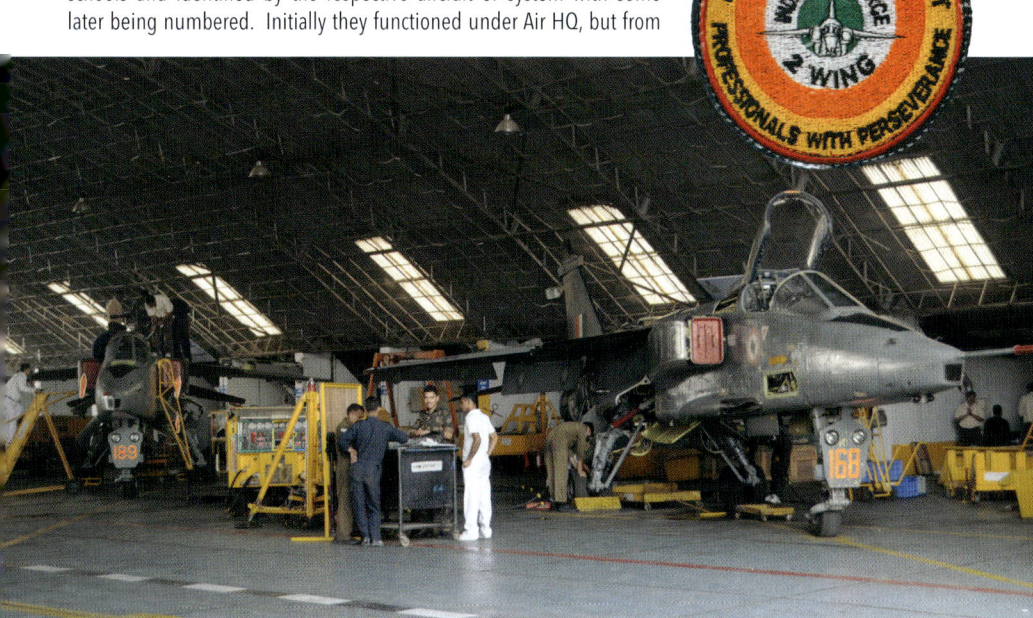

In 1949 a Technical Training College was established at Jalahalli near Bangalore in collaboration with Air Service Training, UK. It was renamed as the Air Force Technical College in 1957 and continues to train officers of the electrical and mechanical streams of aeronautical engineering with students progressing to type specific schools. For its service it was awarded the President Standard in November 2008. From here the graduates can go to type specific training schools. Initially technical training in the IAF was carried out by Mobile Conversion Flights (MCF), however following the recommendations of the La Fontaine Committee; these were converted into Technical Type Training (TETTRA) schools and Technical Type Conversion Units (TTCU). In 1997 the TTCU's were rechristened as TETTRA schools and identified by the respective aircraft or system with some later being numbered. Initially they functioned under Air HQ, but from

▲ Jaguar Tech Flight at Gorakhpur in 2012.

Non Numbered Flying Units

Air Force Technical College, TETTRA, Technical Flights and Base Repair Depots (BRD)

January 2005 they became part of Training Command. The role of the TETTRA is to impart type training to flying and ground duty branches of the IAF. Once qualified they will be allocated to a squadron or a technical flight based at an airbase. These Technical Flights are under the command of HQ Maintenance Command (see page 207) based at Nagpur. This command was set up at Kanpur in January 1955, being the centre of IAF maintenance activities. The command HQ was moved to Nagpur in June 1963 and since inception Maintenance Command has set up 13 Base Repair Depots (BRD) to maintain various types of aircraft and equipment. 1 BRD was set up in August 1948 at Kanpur and has maintained numerous types over the years, recognition of which saw it awarded the President Standard in November 2004. 3 BRD was inaugurated to look after transport and helicopters at Chandigarh in August 1962 (President Standard 15th March 2013) and 4 BRD was set up at Kanpur in 1964 to maintain aero engines (President Standard 11th March 2014). Other notables have included 9 BRD at Pune who have maintained avionics since 1966 and who were awarded the President Standard in January 2011 and 11 BRD who maintain the IAF's MiG-23UB's and MiG-29's at Nasik.

▼ MiG-23UB undergoing deep maintenance at 11 BRD in 2006.

Squadrons, Patches, Heraldry & Artwork of the Indian Air Force: 1932-2016

Air Force Technical College, TETTRA, Technical Flights and Base Repair Depots (BRD)

Non Numbered Flying Units

Air Force Technical College, TETTRA, Technical Flights and Base Repair Depots (BRD)

▲ HQMC badge pictured on their HS-748 at Yelahanka.

200　　Squadrons, Patches, Heraldry & Artwork of the Indian Air Force: 1932-2016

AIR OBSERVATION POST SQUADRONS

The last British AOP squadron in India was 659, with assets in Lahore, Devlali, Razmah, Jullundur and Peshawar. Both India and Pakistan claimed a flight each and used them to commence their own AOP squadrons in support of their respective armies. Number 1 AOP Flight was raised at Lahore on 15th August 1947, followed by 2 AOP Flight which was formed at Devlali on 1st November. Initial equipment consisted of Auster Mk.VI, of which 28 had been left behind by the British and these were later replaced by the Auster AOP9 in the 1950's as the AOP units expanded. The first full AOP squadron, number 659 was raised on 1st June 1958 at Devlali and this was followed by 660 at Nasik Road in 1965. Like the British model, the air force maintained overall control; however the officers were all Indian Army with the ground crew being IAF. During the 1965 War the 2 full squadrons and 5 flights were active on both fronts and impressed several civilian HAL Pushpaks from local flying clubs. 661 squadron was raised in 1967 and another 5 flights followed between 1969 and 1971. The HAL HAOP-27 Krishak entered service in December 1964, followed by the HAL Chetak in March 1969. All three types saw action during the 1971 War providing spotting duties, light communications and CASEVAC. Notably Number 12 (Independent) Air OP Flight were deployed to the Rann of Kutch and acted as forward air controllers for the IAF Hunters, which destroyed a Pakistani Armoured advance at Longewala. After 1971, the Auster was phased out, followed by the Krishak in 1977, leaving the AOP units universally rotary. On 1st November 1986, command passed from the IAF to the IA.

Crest: Shown is the patch of 660 AOP Squadron which shows a Black Kite holding a shell, signifying its role as an artillery spotting unit.

Motto: 'Sarvatra Chaksu / Eyes Everywhere'.

▲ Line up of HAL Krishaks.

▼ HAL Krishak.

Non Numbered Flying Units 201

BASIC FLYING TRAINING SCHOOL

Badge: A roundel in Air Force Blue showing the front view of a Chetak.

Motto: 'Setting Standards'.

The BFTS was established at AFS Bamrauli on 16th December 1987 in order to facilitate the basic training of flight cadets. This was due to substantial increase in the demand for pilots. Original equipment was the HAL HPT-32. Since 1999 the emphasis moved to the training of pilots for the Army, Navy and Coast Guard. In December 2005, this changed again when they received HAL Chetaks in order to train Army Officers.

▼ A BFTS Chetak getting airborne in 2013.

Squadrons, Patches, Heraldry & Artwork of the Indian Air Force: 1932-2016

AIR HEADQUARTERS COMMUNICATION SQUADRON
'PEGASUS'

The squadron was formed on 1st November 1947 at Palam as the Air Headquarters Communication Squadron (RIAF), later dropping the RIAF in favour of IAF when becoming a Republic. Its initial equipment was the Airspeed Oxford and Harvard and its prime role was the conveying of VIPs and visiting foreign heads of states and governments. The Oxford was replaced by the Dakota in 1948 which lasted in service until 1967. Other types operated have been the Devon between 1948 and 1978, the IL-14 from 1955 until 1967, the Viscount from 1956 until 1962, the HS-748 from 1964 to date, the Tu-124 1966 and 1981, the Boeing 737 from 1981 till date, the Mil-8 from 1984 till date and the Embraer 135 from 2006. Since inception the squadron has participated in all post Independence operations beginning with the war in Jammu & Kashmir in 1947, Goa operations in 1960, The Chinese Aggression in 1962, Indo Pak conflicts of 1965, 1971 and 1999 and the IPKF operations in Sri Lanka starting in 1987. They were presented with the President Standard on 11th December 1984.

Crest: In 1962 the President of India awarded the squadron a crest consisting of the Winged Horse 'Pegasus'.

Motto: Seva Aur Suraksha / Service and Safety', was adopted in 1962. Previously it was 'Ba Hikmat, Himmat aur Hifazat/ With Wisdom, Courage and Safety.'

▼ AIRHQCS Embraer 135 gets airborne during Aero India in 2013.

Non Numbered Flying Units   203

Air Headquarters Communication Squadron

▶ PM Indira Gandhi and AIRHQCS crew together before a VIP flight.

▼ WHL Merlin on delivery to the IAF at Stansted, UK. The Merlin never entered service due to a political furore over alleged corruption.

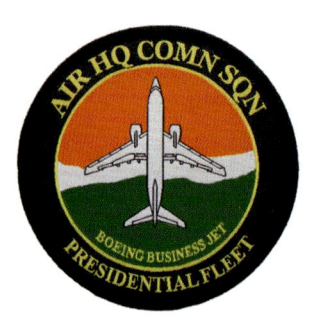

▼ AIRHQCS Mil-8 at Yelahanka in 2013.

▶ The State Emblem of India, the Ashoka, seen on a Mil-8.

204   Squadrons, Patches, Heraldry & Artwork of the Indian Air Force: 1932-2016

HEADQUARTERS CENTRAL AIR COMMAND

The communication flight of Central Air Command was formed in Calcutta on 19th March 1962 and moved to its present home of Allahabad in February 1966. They currently operate the HS-748.

Crest: The crest depicts a Himalayan Eagle holding a spear.

Motto: 'Nigrahya Rasava shastrava / Destruction of the Enemy'.

▲ The CAC HS-748 at Yelahanka in 2001.

▲ The CAC HS-748 at Yelahanka in 2001.

▲ The CAC HQ Flight HS-748 being refuelled at Yelahanka.

Non Numbered Flying Units 205

SOUTHERN AIR COMMAND COMMUNICATIONS FLIGHT

SAC was formed on 19th July 1984 and is based at Trivandrum, where its HQ Flight operates a HS-748.

Crest: A Manta Ray.

Motto: 'Antariksham Prashasmahe / We Command The Space'.

SOUTH WESTERN AIR COMMAND COMMUNICATIONS FLIGHT

SWAC started life as No 1 group at Jodhpur in September 1972, changing its name to SWAC on 23rd July 1980 and in doing so inheriting a large portion of WAC's operational airfields. Later on it took over Pune and Mumbai from CAC and with this increased area moved its HQ to Gandhinagar in 1998. The HQ flight is based at Baroda with a HS-748.

Badge: A dagger with wings.

Motto: 'Jai Shree Veeram / Victory Garlands the Gallant'.
The motto 'Dakshin Paschim Vayu Kaman' is also written on the crest.

EASTERN AIR COMMAND COMMUNICATIONS FLIGHT

103 Communications Flight was raised in Assam with one C-47 in 1956, in order to serve the civil power in Assam. It was home based at Guwahati and Jorhat and the C-47 was augmented by two Austers and later a DHC-3 Otter. The flight moved to Tezpur in 1963 and later Shillong. A HS-748 replaced the Dakota in 1968 and in the 1980's the flight was renamed as the EAC Communications Flight.

Crest: *A double headed mace as used in mythological Meghalaya. (A state in the North East of India).*

Motto: *'Samareshu Parakramah / Valour in Wars'.*

HEADQUARTERS MAINTENANCE COMMAND COMMUNICATIONS FLIGHT

This command was set up at Kanpur on 26th January 1955, being the centre of IAF maintenance activities. The command HQ was moved to Nagpur in June 1963 and from there the Command Flight operates a HS-748.

Badge: *A Himalayan Eagle holding a micrometer.*

Motto: *"Sardava Gagne Charetu / Always Flying High In The Sky".*

◀ H1514 HS-748 HQMC at Yelahanka 2009.

Non Numbered Flying Units   207

HEADQUARTERS TRAINING COMMAND COMMUNICATION FLIGHT

Crest: *A Himalayan Eagle superimposed on a torch. The torch signifying the Light of Knowledge and the Eagle for its swiftness, ferocity and spectacular manner in which it swoops on its quarry.*

Motto: *'Tamaso Ma Jyotirgamaya / O Lord, Lead Me From Darkness To Light'.*

The unit traces its lineage back to the RAF 225 Group Communication Flight which was located at Yelahanka airfield in WWII. In May 1946 the unit moved to nearby HAL airfield in Bangalore and was disbanded. In June 1946 a new unit was formed as No 2 (Indian) Group Communication Flight. This was later changed in August 1947 to No 2 (Training) Group Flight, RIAF. On January 26th 1950 it became the HQ Training Command Flight and moved back to Yelahanka in June 1964. The unit has flown the Harvard, Devon, Dakota and currently operates the HS-748.

▲ HQTC HS-748 at Yelahanka.

▲ HQTC Training Command Logo on an An-32 probably belonging to a TTW An-32.

◄ HQTC steps against their HS-748.

208   Squadrons, Patches, Heraldry & Artwork of the Indian Air Force: 1932-2016

FIXED WING TRAINING FACULTY

The unit traces its history back to 1948 when a Conversion and Training Squadron was set up at Agra with a C-47. It was renamed the Transport Training Wing (TTW) in 1957 and moved to Begumpet Airfield in Hyderabad. No 2 TTW was established at Yelahanka in 1st August 1963 to facilitate the growth in training transport pilots. On January 1st 1968, both TTW's were amalgamated at Yelahanka on the C-47 aircraft. The task of the TTW was to give advanced training to flight cadets in order that they could become transport pilots and navigators in the IAF. In 1974 the C-47's were supplemented by the HS-748, followed by the An-32 in January 1991 and the Dornier 228 in July 1996. The C-47 was withdrawn in 1974 and was followed for a short period of time by the HS-748. (2000). However with the introduction of women pilots in the IAF, the HS-748 had to be re-introduced due to the difficulty in flying the An-32. The unit was renamed as the Fixed Wing Training Faculty in 2000.

Crest: *The unit uses the station crest of Yelahanka as it logo. It has an elephant signifying strength holding a torch in its trunk signifying knowledge.*

Motto: *'Balancha Buddhishcha / Knowledge is Power'.*

▲ Female pilots from the transport stream at Yelahanka in the 1980's.

Non Numbered Flying Units 209

Fixed Wing Training Faculty

▲ Official inspection at the TTW in the 1960's.

210 Squadrons, Patches, Heraldry & Artwork of the Indian Air Force: 1932-2016

Fixed Wing Training Faculty

◀ TTW Dornier 228 at Yelahanka in 1996.

◀ FWTF Dornier 228 at Yelahanka in 2005.

Non Numbered Flying Units 211

FLYING INSTRUCTORS SCHOOL

The FIS was set up on 1st April 1948 at Ambala with the Tiger Moth and Harvard. In 1951 the Percival Prentice was introduced and later withdrawn in 1954. On October 10th 1954 it moved to its present location at Tambaram and the HAL HT2 replaced the Tiger Moth. Later in 1971 the Harvard was replaced by the HAL Kiran and in 1989 the HT2 was replaced by the HPT-32. In 2001 the HAL Chetak was inducted in order to train pilots from the helicopter stream. The FIS was awarded the President Standard on 26th October 1995.

Badge: The crest depicts a Torch with an open fist and clenched fist held upright. The open fist signifies the knowledge imparted and passed on by an instructor to an under training flying instructor. The wings behind the torch depict aviation.

Motto: 'Vidya Danen Vardhate / Knowledge When Imparted Multiplies'.

▲ Instructors and pilots with a HT2 at Tambaram.

▲ FIS HPT-32 at Yelahanka in 1998.

Squadrons, Patches, Heraldry & Artwork of the Indian Air Force: 1932-2016

Flying Instructors School

Non Numbered Flying Units 213

HAWK OPERATIONAL TRAINING SQUADRON
'BRAVEHEARTS'

The unit traces its lineage back to the MiG Operational Flying Training Unit (MOFTU) which stood down at Tezpur in 2007. MOFTU 'A' was selected as the first recipient of the Hawk Mk.132 and stood up at Bidar in July 2008 as the Hawk Operational Training Squadron (HOTS). The aim of the unit is to train and provide fighter pilots for the frontline squadrons. As the Hawk force grew, then so did the Squadrons at Bidar eventually being named as HOTS-B, HOTS-C and HOTS-D with HOTS-A being split off to re-start the OCU in 2015.

Crest: The crest depicts a Hawk and torch against the rising Sun. The Sun being the ancient symbol of radiance and power of the enlightened warrior. The torch represents the torch of knowledge.

Motto: 'Sarva Yudhavisharda / Skilled in All Warfare'.

▼ Hawk Mk.132 at Jaisalmer in 2013.

214 Squadrons, Patches, Heraldry & Artwork of the Indian Air Force: 1932-2016

Hawk Operational Training Squadron

Non Numbered Flying Units   215

HELICOPTER TRAINING SCHOOL
'ARGONAUTS'

The HTS was set up at Palam on April 2nd 1962 with the Bell 47G and was known as the Logistics Support Training Unit. On December 1st of the same year it moved to Bamrauli in Allahabad and in May 1967 it moved to Jodhpur whereupon it changed name to the HTS. At Jodhpur it re-equipped with the HAL Chetak becoming a lodger unit with the AFC and moved to its present home of Hakimpet in October 1973. During its history the HTS has participated in internal Indian relief operations, in the main pertaining to flood relief as a result of cyclones.

Crest: The crest consists of a lighted candle with the sea and sun in the background.

Motto: 'Achievement through Knowledge'.

▲ Inset: Close-up of HTS stencil on a Chetak.   ▲ HTS Chetak at Hakimpet 2001.

216 Squadrons, Patches, Heraldry & Artwork of the Indian Air Force: 1932-2016

IAF FORMATION AEROBATIC TEAM
SURYAKIRAN

The IAF's formation aerobatic team was formed at Bidar on 27th May 1996, under the leadership of Wg Cdr N.K. Malik, who as a Flt Lt had been a member of the Thunderbolts. The deputy team leader, Sqn Ldr A. Mugai had also flown with the Thunderbolts along with one other member of the team. The platform to be used by the new Suryakiran was the locally produced HAL Kiran MK.II, which was used for intermediate jet training at Bidar. A lengthy discussion took place as to the team's name and eventually they settled on the name Suryakiran which translates to Rays of the Sun. Initially the team was to consist of six aircraft; working up to nine after various formations had been practised. Behind the scenes, two aircraft had been painted in different colours, one being post box red and the other being Day-Glo orange. Wg Cdr Malik liked the red version, but was over-ruled by Chief of the Air Staff, ACM S.K. Sareen, who chose the Day-Glo as it would stand out better. By August, eight Kirans had been ferried in from the BRD at Sulur in the new colour scheme along with smoke producing modification. Soon their first public performance occurred when a six ship horizontal display was carried out at Coimbatore on 15th September 1996. Later on October 8th, they performed their first

Crest: *Nine Kiran Mk2 aircraft superimposed on the outline of a 52 squadron Shark.*

Motto: *'Sadaiva Sarvottam / Always the Best'.*

▲ The 1996 Team

Non Numbered Flying Units 217

IAF Formation Aerobatic Team

▲ Suryakiran Kiran MkII air to air.

aerobatic display at Air Force Day at Hindon, near Delhi with six aircraft, which was followed by a seven ship display at the inaugural Aero India at Bangalore in December. Wg Cdr Malik handed over to Murgai in 1998 and under him the team was upgraded to nine aircraft status, performing an aerobatic display for the first time at Palam on 8th October 1998. In March 2001 the team performed overseas for the first time in Sri Lanka to celebrate the 50th Anniversary of the Sri Lanka Air Force. In 2004 a Far East tour was undertaken to Myanmar, Thailand and Singapore with the team travelling 17,000 kms and transiting 10 foreign airbases. Further tours followed in 2007 in order to participate at Langkawi in Malaysia and to China to participate in the 7th Zhuhai Airshow. The team were awarded the Chief of Air Staff Unit Citation in 2004 for its exemplary performance since 1996 and on 1st May 2006, squadron status was conferred upon them when they took on the 52 numberplate. The team were wound down in June 2011 due to a shortage of jet trainers in the IAF. They have been resurrected again in 2015 with four Hawk aircraft and performed their first public display on Air Force Day at Hindon.

IAF Formation Aerobatic Team

▲ 2001 Team at Aero India.

▲ 2007 Team at Aero India.

▲ Welcoming sign to the Suryakiran HQ at Bidar.

Non Numbered Flying Units   219

IAF Formation Aerobatic Team

▲ 2009 Team at Aero India.

▶ 1998 Team at Aero India.

▼ Line up of team helmets in the crew room at Yelahanka in 2005.

220 Squadrons, Patches, Heraldry & Artwork of the Indian Air Force: 1932-2016

IAF Formation Aerobatic Team

▲ New team at Air Force Day, Hindon 2015.

▼ New team colours resplendent on this Hawk Mk.132 at Hindon 2015.

Non Numbered Flying Units   221

JET BOMBER CONVERSION UNIT

The JBCU was established at Agra in 1958 on the Canberra in order to facilitate the training of large numbers of pilots and navigators that were needed to man the expanding bomber fleet. They fulfilled a dual role in that they primarily were a training establishment that in time of war could step up as extra bomber formation. During the 1965 War they flew several CAS missions alongside 5 and 35 squadrons against enemy airfields including Mianwali, Sargodha and Peshawar, and their commanding officer, Sqn Ldr Peter Gautam was awarded the MvC for his actions during the conflict. During the 1971 War the unit again was placed on operations and conducted interdiction over West Pakistan, losing one Canberra and crew on the night of 4th December 1971. They were numberplated in 1979 as the Canberra fleet had been cut, aircrew training then being taken over by the remaining squadrons.

Crest: *Two Flamingos flying in formation.*

Motto: *'Sushikshit Susajjit / Well Trained is Well Armed.'*

▼ Wg Cdr Pete Gautam on the left with a JBCU Canberra.

MIG OPERATIONAL FLYING TRAINING UNIT

MOFTU was formed on 15th December 1986 at Tezpur on the MiG-21FL and MiG-21U. The primary role of the unit was to instruct operational flying training to pilots inducted into the fighter stream. MOFTU was the largest fighter-flying establishment in the Indian Air Force and consisted of two squadrons, Alpha and Bravo. The unit has stood up twice for operational deployments in time of tension with Pakistan. The first being Operation Brass Tacks in January 1987 and more recently Operation Parakram in May 2002. Each time they despatched aircraft to operate at bases in Western Air Command, where they stood alert on operational readiness platforms. The unit ceased to exist in September 2007, when all its aircraft were transferred to the OCU at Bagdoghra.

Crest: The official unit emblem depicts a Hawk (signifying the instructor), leading a fledgling (signifying the student).

Motto: 'Sarva Yudhavisharda / All Skilled in Warfare'

◀ MOFTU Instructors and Pilots at Tezpur in 2002.

◀ MOFTU MiG-21FL taxies in at Tezpur after a sortie in 2002.

Non Numbered Flying Units 223

MiG Operational Flying Training Unit

▲ MOFTU Crest development.

▼ Nose artwork on a MOFTU MiG-21FL in 1998.

224 Squadrons, Patches, Heraldry & Artwork of the Indian Air Force: 1932-2016

NATIONAL DEFENCE ACADEMY/AIR FORCE TRAINING TEAM

The Air Force Training Team (AFTT) was formed in 1956 at the National Defence Academy (NDA) in Khadakwasla, 17 kms South West of Pune. Since conception the AFTT has used mainly Gliders such as the Sedbergh T-21B, EON Baby, EON Olympic, HAL Rohini and HAL Ardha, to give the NDA students some flying experience. Today the NDA accepts about 300 students per annum from all three services and the 60 or so IAF Cadets are trained in the basics of military aviation. The Super Dimona was inducted into the fleet in 2001 and the cadets fly eight sorties on these under the supervision of IAF pilots that have passed the Flying Instructors Course.

▲ Super Dimona airborne near Pune.

NAVIGATOR TRAINING SCHOOL

Part of the 12 squadron role whilst at Risalpur in 1946, was to train navigators with their six Airspeed Oxfords. In November 1946 the units Oxfords were sent to Ambala where an embryo Navigation School was set up. The Navigation Training School was then transferred in 1949 to Jodhpur as part of the Air Force College on the C-47. The Air Signallers School was amalgamated into it in 1963 and it was renamed the Navigation and Signals School (NSS). Its task was to train navigators and signallers not only for the IAF, but the Indian Navy and foreign states such as Egypt and Iraq. In January 1968 it moved to its current location at Begumpet near Hyderabad, being the fourth of the TC air stations in the Hyderabad area. In February 1972, the C-47s were replaced by the HS-748. On 12th March 2003 the NSS was renamed as the Navigational Training School.

Crest: *An Albatross signifying long range navigation over a set of geometric dividers and lightning bolts.*

Motto: *'Sarvada Lakshyam Prapyate / Ever Achieving Their Goal'.*

▼ Navigation Training School HS-748 at Yelahanka in 2005.

226 Squadrons, Patches, Heraldry & Artwork of the Indian Air Force: 1932-2016

OPERATIONAL CONVERSION UNIT
'THE YOUNG ONES'

The OCU was raised on 1st October 1966 at Jamnagar with the Hunter F56A, and was initially known as the Operational Training Unit (OTU). Its purpose was to ensure the smooth transition of young pilots from training into the front line squadrons. During the 1971 Indo-Pak War it operated a four aircraft detachment from Jaisalmer and was temporarily known as 122 Squadron. On the 5th December 1971 a regiment of Pakistan Army T55 Tanks crossed the border near Tanot, with the aim of capturing Jaisalmer by sun down. Following a request to help from the Indian Army, the detachment destroyed or damaged 29 tanks in 48 hours. This action stopping the enemy advance in its tracks and earning the unit the battle honour of 'Longewala'. During the 1971 War the OCU flew 256 sorties and apart from Longewala also carried out interdiction strikes against enemy railheads and counter air strikes against airfields and radar stations. Flying training resumed in February 1972 and in April 1975 the unit moved to Kalaikunda and was renamed the OCU. On 31st March 1991 the OCU was numberplated and all its assets were transferred to 20 Squadron. On 1st January 1998 it was resurrected at Chabua to implement the MOFT Syllabus. The unit was temporarily numberplated in 2013 when the MiG-21FL was retired, but has now been resurrected on the BAe Hawk.

Crest: The OCU Crest depicts 3 Himalayan Eagles flying through lightning. The Eagles depict ferocity, aggressiveness and fearlessness and by flying in formation they depict the high level of integrity, faith and mutual co-operation that exists amongst its members. The unit name of 'The Young Ones' refers to the junior pilots/aspiring Eaglets in their ranks.

Motto: 'Only Through Hard Work and High Level of Training Will Success Be Achieved'.

Battle Honours:

Indo-Pak Conflict 1971 (West Pakistan)
Pak Offensive (Rajasthan Conflict)
Longewala

▼ Hawk Mk.132 at Yelahanka.

Non Numbered Flying Units   227

Operational Conversion Unit

▲ The unit HQ at Chabua in 2001.

◀ Tastefully decorated blast shield at Chabua reflecting the unit's proudest moment.

228 Squadrons, Patches, Heraldry & Artwork of the Indian Air Force: 1932-2016

Operational Conversion Unit

Non Numbered Flying Units   229

PARACHUTE TRAINING SCHOOL
'SKYHAWKS'

Crest: *The Crest depicts a deployed parachute bringing down a supply container with wings attached.*

Motto: *'Saahas Kaushalam Balam / Courage, Skill, Strength'.*

In October 1941 the 50th Independent Para Brigade was formed in Delhi together with an Air Landing School. In 1942 the ALS moved to Chaklala and was re-christened as no. 3 Parachute Training School. Paratroopers were initially given training on Wellingtons from 215 Squadron RAF, later moving onto other types such as the Dakota, Valentia, Hudson and Halifax. In 1947 during partition, 12 Para Instructors along with 38 Para Jumper Instructors left the unit and moved to Agra. This was the basis of a revised Parachute Training School and they received their first Dakota in 1949. In 1963 they converted onto the C-119 and flew support missions during the 1965 War. In 1971 they forward deployed to Phaphamu and carried out the training of pilots from the transport stream on day and night operations. They themselves also participated in the acclaimed Para drop over Tangail on 11th December 1971. The unit have also participated in operations over the Siachen Glacier, Sri Lanka and Operations Pawan and Cactus. They were awarded the President Standard in November 1994 and converted onto the An-32 on 10th July 1984. Qualified Para Jumper Instructors from the unit formed the Akash Ganga Sky Diving team on 9th August 1987 and they have performed at various events all over India. A second team known as the Air Devils were formed in 1988 by officers and men from other branches that are members of the IAF Adventure Cell.

▼ PTS C-119 at Agra 1970's.

Parachute Training School

Non Numbered Flying Units 231

TACTICS AND COMBAT DEVELOPMENT ESTABLISHMENT

On 1st February 1971 the GOI sanctioned the formation of the Tactics and Combat Development and Training Squadron (TCDTS) which was formed at Adampur with four MiG-21FL's and four Su-7s. The primary task of the unit was the study and evolution of tactical procedures for various aircraft, their implementation in the form of standard operating procedures and the training of pilots in those new operational doctrines and tactics. Personnel were given free hand to explore various combos of formations including 10 aircraft melees of four attackers, two escorts and four bouncers. In May 1971 the unit was moved to Ambala and was tasked with developing specialized night attack missions. From there they commenced counter air missions against Pakistani airfields at night using single aircraft, a tactic that they had themselves developed. These continued for several nights

▼ MiG-21FL of TACDE in the late 1970's.

until the unit changed its role to on the 8th December when daytime counter air strikes, interdiction and close air support missions began. The squadrons assets were split with the Su-7s being used for bombing and the MiG-21FL's for escort. By the end of hostilities they had flown 174 day sorties and 119 sorties by night, with the loss of one aircraft and pilot. In December 1972 the unit moved to Jamnagar and changed its name to the Tactics and Air Combat Development Establishment (TACDE). At this time flight commanders from the operational fighter squadrons were invited to TACDE for ad-hoc courses on the doctrines developed by the resident unit. These courses eventually developed into a training syllabus in which optimum flying techniques and tactics were developed which lead to the creation of the 'Blue Book' containing tactics and the 'Red Book' for pilot attack instruction. In May 1973 this developed into the first Fighter Combat Leader's Course taking place which continues to this day. Over time other courses were developed including the Fighter Strike Leader course, the Master Fighter Controller Course and the Helicopter Combat Leader Course. In June 1982 the MiG-21FL and Su-7 were phased out and the unit was re-equipped with the MiG-21M and BIS. In June 1994 the MiG-21M was phased out and its place taken by the MiG-27. In December 1997 TACDE moved to its current home of Gwalior and a purpose built Air Combat Maneuvering Range was set up. In the mid 2000's it converted onto the MiG-21 Bison and continues to operate that type alongside the Su-30MKI which replaced the MiG-27 in 2009.

Crest: The unit crest consists of a pair of clashing swords bracketing a winged torch on a red background. The swords indicate the willingness of combat and the burning torch symbolizes the teaching of air to air combat. The red background signifies the bloodied battleground. Spaced equally around the swords are seven stars which symbolize astro navigation and capabilities to conduct night operations.

Motto: 'Tejas Tejaswi Namaham' which translates to 'I am the glory of the glorious'.

Non Numbered Flying Units   233

Tactics And Combat Development Establishment

234 Squadrons, Patches, Heraldry & Artwork of the Indian Air Force: 1932-2016

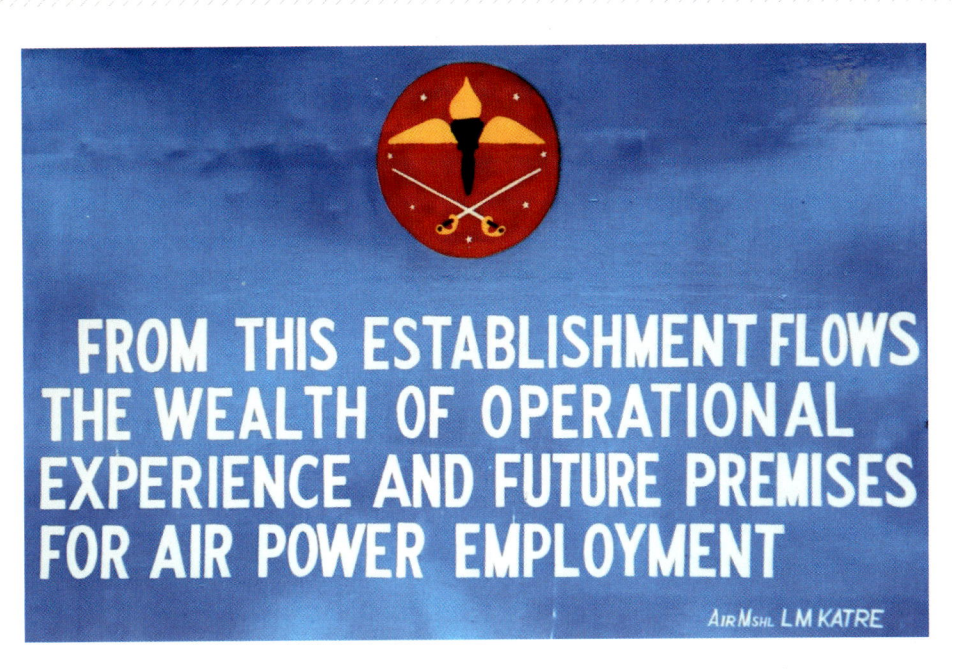

Tactics And Combat Development Establishment

> **FROM THIS ESTABLISHMENT FLOWS THE WEALTH OF OPERATIONAL EXPERIENCE AND FUTURE PREMISES FOR AIR POWER EMPLOYMENT**
>
> Air Mshl LM KATRE

◀ ▲ Building artwork.

Non Numbered Flying Units

Tactics And Combat Development Establishment

236 Squadrons, Patches, Heraldry & Artwork of the Indian Air Force: 1932-2016

TARGET TUG FLIGHT
'BANNERS'

The TTF was raised at Kalaikunda with Hunters in 1972. In 1978 a sister unit was formed at Kalaikunda known as the Chakor Pilotless Target Aircraft Squadron (CPTA) flying a locally made version of the Northrop Chukar, known as the Chakor. This remotely operated vehicle is a small lightweight target for anti aircraft gunnery, surface to air missile training and weapons evaluation. The CPTA squadron was merged into the TTF on 14th August 1998 and became its 'A' Flight. By then the Chakor was reaching the end of its operational career and was to be replaced by the Indigenous RPV known as the Lakshya (True Aim). The TTF were the last IAF unit to fly the Hunter, retiring them in 2001.

Badge: An Eagle holding a target sleeve.

▲ TTF Pilots in front of a Hunter T66 at KKD in 1999.

▲ Withdrawn Hunter T66 with high viz stripes at KKD in 1999.
▶ Starboard side view of a TTF badge on a Hunter T66.

▲ Port side view of TTF badge on a Hunter F56.

Non Numbered Flying Units   237

TARGET TUG UNIT

Badge: An Eagle atop an Anchor with crossed Swords signifying the IAF, IN and IA.

The unit was first established as the Target Tug Flight at Jamnagar in 1951 with the Dakota. In May 1969, the TTF was divided into 1 Target Tug Unit and 2 Target Tug Unit, which were based at Cochin and Palam respectively. As the name suggests their main role was target towing for the air defence element of both the Indian Navy (from Cochin) and the Indian Army (from Palam). In June 1985, both units were re-equipped with the Canberra B(I).58 and later relocated, with 1 TTU going to Pune and 2 TTU to Agra in November 1987. At this point their roles changed from target towing for the Navy/Army to banner towing for air to air firing requirements of the IAF. The Navy/Army requirements had previously been passed to 6 squadron that had received specially modified Canberra TT418 aircraft with the pylon mounted Rushton winch and target. On 15th June 1992, a unified Target Tug Unit was raised at Agra by merging 1 TTU, 2 TTU and TT Flight of 6 squadron. With the merger the unit took on the banner, sleeve and Ruston Target towing for all three services. Banner towing ceased on 31st March 1996 and target towing assets were reduced to four Canberra TT418 aircraft. The TTU was finally merged into 106 squadron at Agra on 1st August 1997.

QUASI-MILITARY FLYING UNITS

Several mixed military/civil units exist that operate aircraft. These are all involved in the development and manufacturing of aircraft and systems.

HINDUSTAN AERONAUTICS LIMITED

The Hindustan Aircraft Company was set up on a new site in Bangalore on 23rd December 1940. Initially it was a private limited company with its backers being the Government of Mysore, Indian Industrialist Seth Walchand Hirachand and American Douglas Pawley, who was a director of Harlow Aircraft of Alhambra, California. The first aircraft to be manufactured at the plant was the Harlow PC-5A, the first flight of which took place on 29th July 1941. This was followed by a locally designed 10 seat G-1 Glider, the Curtiss Hawk 75A fighter and the Vultee V-12D dive bomber. By 1943 events forced the production cycle to cease at the HAL factory, as the US Army Air Force negotiated with the GOI to use it as a repair and maintenance facility supporting the 10th Air Force in the China, Burma, India theatre, thus becoming the 84th Air Depot. The USAAF began shipping in plant and equipment, turning HAL into a prime repair depot. The workforce was also expanded and trained with the Americans

▼ HAL HT-2 aircraft production line, seen here in May 1955.

Squadrons, Patches, Heraldry & Artwork of the Indian Air Force: 1932-2016

▲ The HAOP-27 Krishak assembly line seen here on 26 October 1967.

◀ HAL Cheetah and Chetak helicopters lined up in May 1969.

paying all the wages. Every US type in theatre was serviced at the depot, including the engines and accessories. At war end, the USAAF gave up the management of the plant and it came under the control of the GOI who set about reducing the workforce from the wartime level of 14,000 to peacetime 3,000. The GOI decided to make HAL the centre of a peacetime nationalised aircraft industry, although initially much of their business was in support of the IAF. In 1948 HAL rebuilt circa 40 B-24 Liberators that had remained at various maintenance units around India for the IAF and this was followed up by numerous C-47 Dakotas that were taken by the IAF and newly formed civilian operators. New aircraft were purchased by the newly independent GOI and usually as part of the deal, licence production by way of local assembly and later full manufacturing was

Hindustan Aeronautics Limited

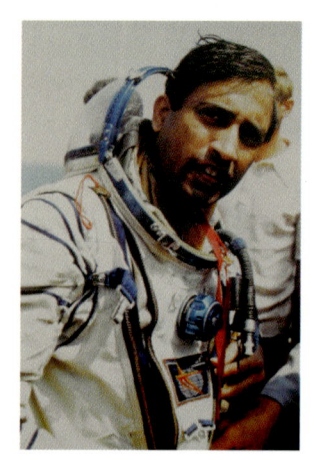

Wg Cdr Rakesh Sharma, Chief Test Pilot of HAL was the first Indian to travel in space when he flew aboard Soyuz T-11, launched April 3, 1984, as part of the Intercosmos programme.

to take place in India. The first of the types to go through this process was the Percival Prentice in 1948, followed by the Vampire in February 1952, the Gnat in November 1959, the HS-748 from a new factory at Kanpur, set up by the IAF (known as the Aircraft Manufacturing Depot and merged into HAL in 1964) in 1961, the Dornier 228 in 1986, the Jaguar in 1981 and the Hawk 132 in 2008. Aeronautics India was set up in August 1963 at Ojhar, near Nasik to licence produce the MiG-21 and this became the MiG Complex of a rechristened Hindustan Aeronautics Ltd in October 1964, going onto make over 500 MiG-21's and 165 MiG-27's over the next 30 years. The first indigenously designed aircraft at HAL was the HT-2 primary trainer which first flew on 5th August 1951. This was followed by the HF-24 Marut jet fighter designed in house by Kurt Tank, which flew for the first time on 17th June 1961 and then went onto serve with three squadrons during the 1971 Indo-Pak War. Another HAL designed product was the HJT-16 Kiran primary jet trainer, which first flew on 4th September 1964. HAL also designed and manufactured light aircraft, starting with the HUL-26 Pushpak primary trainer which flew first on 28th September 1958 and which was to be used by civil flying clubs. The HAOP-27 Krishak, an Air Observation Post (AOP) four seat aircraft which flew for the first time in November 1959 and then the HA-31 Basant,

HAL IJT (later Sitara) prototype in original colour scheme at Aero India in 2005.

242 Squadrons, Patches, Heraldry & Artwork of the Indian Air Force: 1932-2016

Hindustan Aeronautics Limited

▲ HAL Sitara at Aero India in 2011.

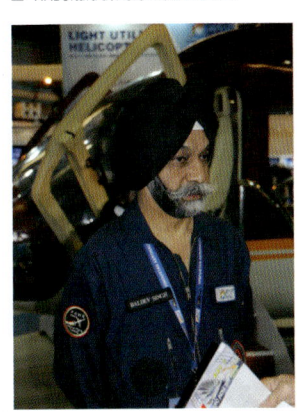

▲ The late Chief Test Pilot of HAL, Sqn Ldr Baldev Singh at Aero India in 2013.

agricultural aircraft which was flown first on 30th April 1972. The HPT-32 primary trainer was manufactured at Kanpur and first flew in March 1984 and replaced the HT-2 in service. HAL got its first rotary experience in 1965, when the GOI signed up for licence production of the Sud Alouette III and Alouette II. The first HAL produced items rolled off the line in 1970 and were christened the Chetak and Cheetah in Indian Military service. Later improved variants like the Cheetal and Lancer were developed for service. The licence production of the Su-30MKI was signed in June 1994 and this has ensured that production of fighter aircraft has continued at the MiG Complex at Ojhar. Today HAL is very busy at its various plants, servicing aircraft of the Indian Military and manufacturing new types such as the Dhruv Advanced Light Helicopter and its attack version known as the Rudra (first flights 20/8/92 and 16/08/07 respectively), Light Combat Helicopter (first flight 29/3/10), Tejas Light Combat Aircraft (first flight 04/01/01) and the HJT-36 Sitara Intermediate Jet Trainer (first flight 07/03/03). HAL maintains its own flight departments for fixed wing and rotary and these pilots are primarily ex Indian Military.

Quasi-Military Flying Units   243

Hindustan Aeronautics Limited

◀ HAL Rudhra which is a weaponised Dhruv, at Aero India in 2013.

244　Squadrons, Patches, Heraldry & Artwork of the Indian Air Force: 1932-2016

Hindustan Aeronautics Limited

▲ HAL's new product, the Light Combat Helicopter at Aero India in 2015.

▼ The Seychelles Air Force's Dornier 228K aircraft gifted by India, which is part of the SAF's fleet of three aircraft. Pictured here at Aero India 2013.

Quasi-Military Flying Units 245

CENTRE FOR AIRBORNE SYSTEMS (CABS)

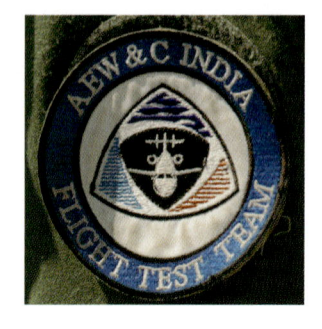

CABS, a laboratory of the Defence Research and Development Organisation (DRDO) was set up in Bangalore in 1991 in order to develop the Airborne Surveillance Platform for the IAF. Two HS-748 were modified in Bangalore and thereafter they commenced a series of highly challenging trials on an airframe that had extensive structural modifications including the addition of a rotor dome and vertical pylon. The modified aircraft first flew in January 1987 and ASTE were able to establish the handling performances and flight characteristics of the modified aircraft. Substantial progress had been made in airborne early warning active and passive detection, when sadly the project came to an abrupt end when the aircraft crashed at Arrakonam on 11th January 1999, killing all onboard including four flight test crew and four scientists. The surviving aircraft was later used in testing the Tejas radar, having a fighter nose cone fitted. Three Embraer 145's were ordered by India in order to be fitted with an airborne Active Electronically Scanned Array (AESA) developed by CABS. The first aircraft arrived in August 2012 and since then integration of the AESA and other systems has been taking place.

▼ Embraer 145 of CABS at Aero India in 2013.

246 Squadrons, Patches, Heraldry & Artwork of the Indian Air Force: 1932-2016

Centre For Airborne Systems (CABS)

▲ The ill fated HS-748 which crashed on 11th January 1999, seen in better times at Aero India in 1998.

▲ The remaining CABS HS-748 fitted with a LCA nose at Aero India in 2001.

▲ CABS Flight crew at Aero India in 2001.

Quasi-Military Flying Units 247

AERONAUTICAL DEVELOPMENT AGENCY

The Aeronautical Development Agency (ADA) was set up in 1985 as a society under the control of the Ministry of Defence to act as program manager for the Light Combat Aircraft (LCA) which was being developed in India. The ADA went about putting together a team of designers drawn from HAL, the National Aerospace Laboratories, the IAF and the Indian Space Research Laboratory (ISRO), to come up with a proposal. After discussions at Air HQ, an Air Staff Requirement for a multi-role fighter aircraft was issued in late 1985. In 1994, the National Flight Test Centre (NFTC) was formed in order to handle the test flying of the LCA. This was to be staffed by IAF Pilots from ASTE, which resulted in a certain amount of bad feeling from HAL, who were bitterly opposed to the idea of separate test pilots just for the LCA Project. After a prolonged development the first LCA prototype was flown on 4th January 2001, piloted by Wg Cdr Rajiv Kothiyal. The LCA was officially christened as the Tejas on 4th May 2003 and is due to enter squadron service with number 45 in 2016.

▲ KH2004, the fourth prototype LCA at Aero India in 2011.

Aeronautical Development Agency

▲ Two Tejas Test Pilots at Aero India in 2011.

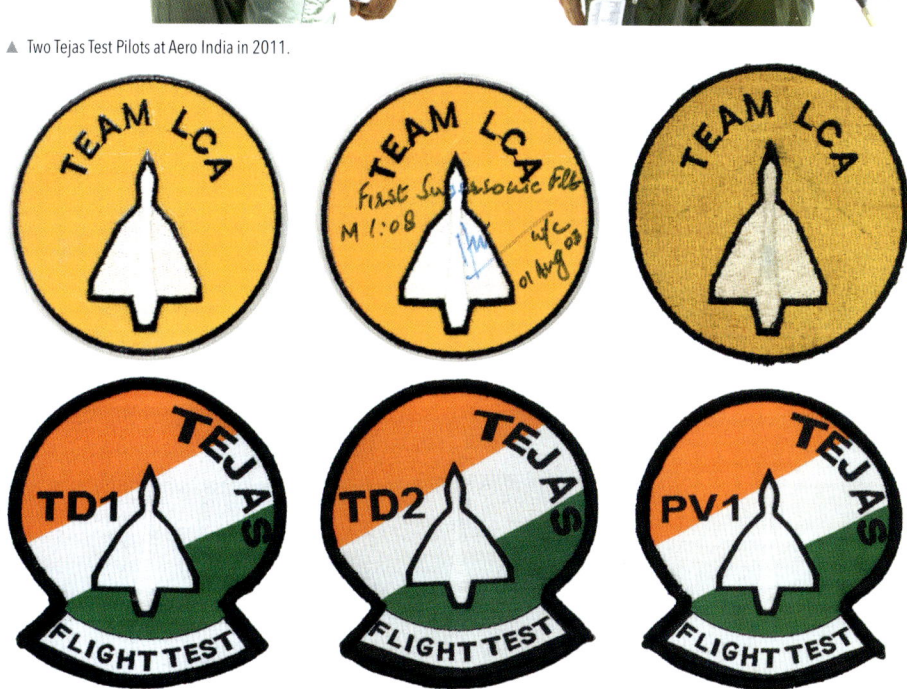

Quasi-Military Flying Units 249

Aeronautical Development Agency

▲ Tejas Test Pilot after a display at Aero India in 2011.

250 ⊙ Squadrons, Patches, Heraldry & Artwork of the Indian Air Force: 1932-2016

MISCELLANEOUS PATCHES

The miscellaneous section includes all other patches. These consist of wings (most airbases are numbered starting at No 1 Srinagar to at least No 49 Naliya), exercise patches, communications, radar units, generic type qualification, unmanned aerial vehicles and missiles. The IAF Missile units were first raised in 1965 to accommodate the SAM2 and were initially numbered in the existing squadron sequence and fill many of the gaps. Examples include numbers 34, 46, 50 (old), 53, 58, 62, 63, 64, 68, 69, 70, 72 and 74. Nowadays they have their own range with the S-123M Pechora Squadrons (SA-3 Goa) being numbered in the 22xx range, the OSA-AK (SAM-8) being numbered in the 225x range and finally the 19K310 (Igla) being numbered in the 23xx range.

Miscellaneous Patches

WINGS

▲ Artwork on a hangar door at Air Force Station Chabua

252 Squadrons, Patches, Heraldry & Artwork of the Indian Air Force: 1932-2016

MISSILE UNITS

Miscellaneous Patches

▲ Pechora transporter at Gwalior in 2003.

PECHORA

नं. 2201 स्क्वाड्रन
सङ्गमे जयते शूरः

DEFENDERS
2202 SQN AF

SILVER ARROWS
LAUNCH TO KILL

THUNDERBOLTS
2207 SQN

SILVER ARROWS
2203 SQUADRON
LAUNCH TO KILL

THUNDERBOLTS
2207 SQN

KILLERS
2210 SQN

SA-III
SHOOT TO KILL

Miscellaneous Patches 253

Miscellaneous Patches

254 Squadrons, Patches, Heraldry & Artwork of the Indian Air Force: 1932-2016

Miscellaneous Patches

▲ OSA-AK belonging to 2253 Squadron (Ardroite) in 2003.

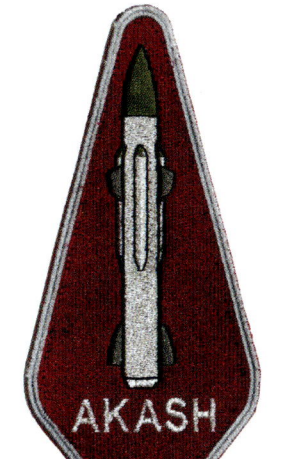

Miscellaneous Patches 255

Miscellaneous Patches

EXERCISES

Miscellaneous Patches

Miscellaneous Patches

COMMUNICATIONS & RADAR UNITS

Miscellaneous Patches

GENERIC MiG-21

GENERIC MiG-23/27

Miscellaneous Patches 259

Miscellaneous Patches

GENERIC MiG-29

260 Squadrons, Patches, Heraldry & Artwork of the Indian Air Force: 1932-2016

Miscellaneous Patches

GENERIC Mil-35

Miscellaneous Patches

GENERIC M2000

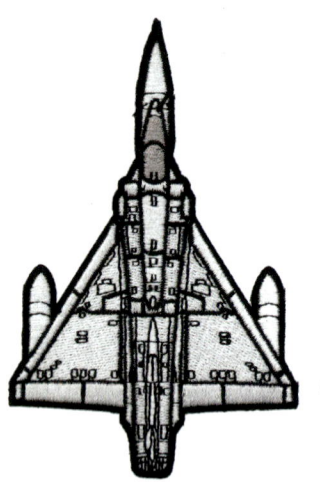

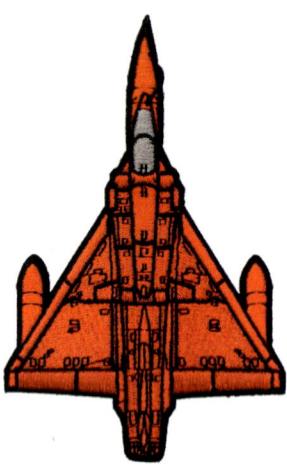

MISCELLANEOUS

Miscellaneous Patches

Miscellaneous Patches · 263

Miscellaneous Patches

GENERIC SU-30

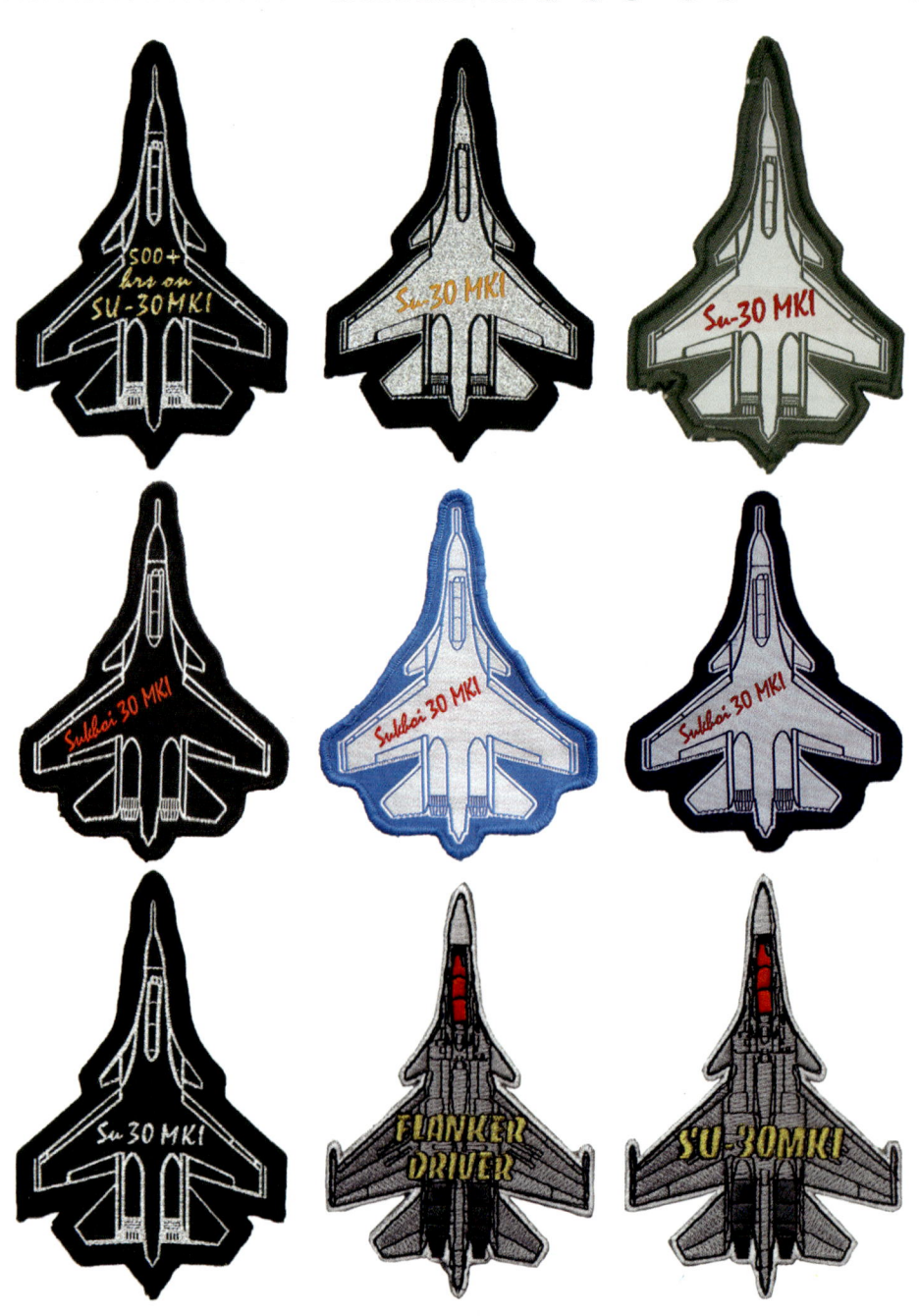

Miscellaneous Patches

Miscellaneous Patches

UNMANNED AERIAL VEHICLES (UAV)

▶ Chakor Flight artwork at TTF building at Kalaikunda in 1999. (see TTF page 237)

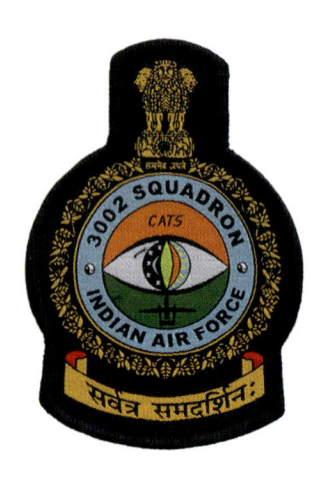

266 Squadrons, Patches, Heraldry & Artwork of the Indian Air Force: 1932-2016

Miscellaneous Patches

LATE ADDITIONS

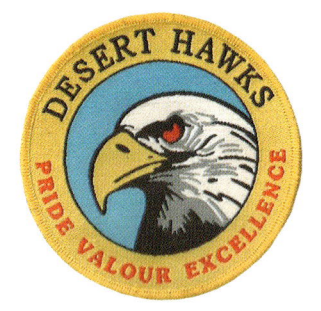

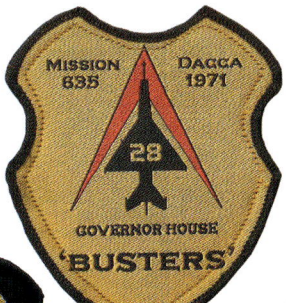

- DESERT HAWKS — PRIDE VALOUR EXCELLENCE
- FIGHTING FOURTEEN — BULLS
- FEROCIOUS FIVE — TUSKERS
- VAJRA WOLF PACK
- Desert Tigers — Courage Valor Firmness
- INDIAN AIR FORCE — PUNE PIONEERS
- 16 COBRAS
- MISSION 635 — DACCA 1971 — 28 — GOVERNOR HOUSE — 'BUSTERS'
- LEAN MEAN FIGHTING MACHINE — LIGHTS FORK DROP KICK — MIGHTY MIG-21
- 314 TRU — INDIAN AIR FORCE — THAR SHIELD
- MiG 21 Bis

Miscellaneous Patches 267

GLOSSARY

AFC	Air Force College
AATU	Aircraft & Armament Testing Unit. Forerunner of ASTE
AIRHQCS	Air Headquarters Communication Squadron at Palam
ALG	Air Landing Ground. A remote landing strip run by the IAF with minimal facilities
AOP	Air Observation Post. Used in the context of Army co-operation
ATGM	Anti Tank Guided Missile. (Type SS11)
BKT	Bakshi Ka Talab airbase in Lucknow
BRD	Base Repair Depot
BRTF	Border Roads Task Force. An Army organisation that constructs and maintains roads in the border areas
CAC	Central Air Command based at Allahabad
CAP	Combat Air Patrol
CAS	Close Air Support or Counter Air Strike (actions against enemy airfields)
CASEVAC	Casualty Evacuation
DRDO	Defence Research Development Organisation
DSO	Distinguished Service Order (UK)
EAC	Eastern Air Command based at Shillong
FAC	Forward Air Controller
F/O	Flying officer
Flt Lt	Flight Lieutenant
GARUD	Special Forces unit of the IAF formed in 2004
GOI	Government of India
HAL	Hindustan Aeronautics Ltd
IA	Indian Army
IAF	Indian Air Force
IAFVR	Indian Air Force Volunteer Reserve.
IN	Indian Navy
IPKF	Indian Peace Keeping Force in Sri Lanka
J&K	State of Jammu and Kashmir
KKD	Kalaikunda air base in Bengal
MOFT	MiG Operational Flying Training
MR	Maritime Reconnaissance
MU	Maintenance Unit
MvC	Maha Vir Chakra. India's second highest award equivalent to DSO
Naxalite	A Communist Guerrilla group operating in West Bengal since 1967
NCC	National Cadet Corp
NEFA	North East Frontier Agency. Used by the British and GOI until 1972 when it became Arunachal Pradesh
NSG	National Security Guard. (Indian Special Forces)
NWFP	North West Frontier Province. A province of British India
OCU	Operational Conversion Unit
ONGC	Oil and Natural Gas Corporation formed in 1956 by the GOI
Operation Black Tornado	Operation by the NSG to flush out terrorist infiltrators in Mumbai on 29.11.08
Operation Brasstacks	A major troop mobilisation in Rajasthan which took place in 1986

Glossary

Operation Cactus	1988 intervention by Indian Military in the Maldives following a coup attempt
Operation Cactus Lily	Indian Air Force code name for operations in East Pakistan, December 1971
Operation Meghdoot	Indian Armed Forces action launched in April 1984 to gain control of the Siachen Glacier
Operation Mop	1953 Operation in NEFA to counter tribal groups
Operation Parakram	Indo-Pak standoff along the Line of Control in J&K in 2001-2002, following an attack on the Indian Parliament
Operation Pawan	Code name for the IPKF action against the Tamil Tigers in Sri Lanka in 1987
Operation Polo	Police action taken by Indian Armed forces in September 1948 to integrate Hyderabad into the State of India
Operation Rakshak	An anti terrorist exercise that took place in Tamil Nadu in 2009
Operation Rhino	Indian Military Operation against the United Liberation Front of Assam
Operation Safed Sagar	IAF Operation to support IA on the ground against infiltration from Pakistan in Kargil during 1999
Operation Vijay	Indian Liberation of Goa in 1961
PAF	Pakistan Air Force
P/O	Pilot Officer
PTS	Parachute Training School
PvC	Param Vir Chakra. India's highest gallantry medal equivalent to Victoria Cross (UK) and Congressional Medal of Honour (USA)
RS&U	Repair & Salvage Unit
SAR	Search & Rescue
Sqn Ldr	Squadron Leader
RUF	Revolutionary United Front. A group of rebels active in Sierra Leone in 1993
SAC	Southern Air Command based at Trivandrum
SEAC	South East Asia Command. A British Unit that oversaw all RAF and IAF operations during WWII
SHBO	Special Heliborne Operations
SLAIS	Special Low Attack Instructors School, Ranchi
SWAC	South West Air Command. Headquartered at Gandhinagar
TAC-R	Tactical Reconnaissance
TETTRA	Technical Type Training School
TTF	Target Tug Flight
TTU	Target Tug Unit
TTW	Transport Training Wing
VIP	Very Important Person
VrC	Vir Chakra gallantry medal equivalent to Distinguished Flying Cross (UK)
WAC	Western Air Command based in Delhi
WHL	Westland Helicopters later to Agusta Westland Helicopters
1 SFTS	No 1 Senior Flying training School established at Ambala on 23rd October 1940
151 OTU	Formed in July 1942 at Risalpur to train Indian Fighter Pilots
152 OTU	Formed in October 1942 at Peshawar to train Indian Bomber Pilots

▲ 29 Squadron mural at its homebase in SWAC.

▲ Nice night shot of a Jaguar IM taken in 2012.